ACTION POTENTIAL

ACTION POTENTIAL

The Secrets of Superlearners

Vivian Mougios, PhD

For permission requests, please contact
vivian@drmougios.com.

Published by Amazon – Kindle Direct Publishing
Printed in the United States.
ISBN-13: 9781731194138

To my greatest teachers: My husband, children, siblings, and parents. I feel blessed to receive such profound, unconditional love and support from you each day.

Acknowledgments

Admittedly, it has taken all my executive functioning skills, grit, and growth mindset to bring this book to fruition. The journey has been fraught with setbacks, blessed with miracles, and humbled by wonderful encounters.

To my husband, William Brett, and children, Thalia and Leander. Your love and devotion provide daily reminders of what matters most.

Thank you to my parents, George and Christine, and my siblings, Larry and Marina. Your influence and unconditional love knows no bounds.

A special thanks to Ken and Gerry Brett. The monogrammed pen will finally bear its ink on the first copy.

I want to extend an important thank you to Christiana Gozo. You formed the backbone for this project and helped translate my ideas into words.

A profound thank you to Jack Schlossberg. Your academic evolution has been an inspiration to Action Potential. E Tan E Epi Tas!

Thank you to Dr. Katherine Eiges, you were tremendous in your dedication at the final hour of publication.

Deepest gratitude to my assistant, Christina Galese. You carried this project to the finish line, and for that I am forever grateful.

To all the schools, parents, and educators whom I have had the pleasure and fortune to learn from–I thank you and remain humbled by your devotion to learning.

And finally, I thank all the students whom I have had the fortune to work with throughout my tenure. You have made my life's work meaningful beyond words.

Table of Contents

Introduction

Throughout the course of my work in the field of neuropsychology, education, and child development, one of the most common questions asked by parents, teachers, and educators alike is, what cognitive competencies enable children to learn most successfully? Plainly, **what do students need in order to be optimal learners?** Applying the knowledge of neuroscience and brain development, the aim of this book is to answer this question with the intent to create a framework that is tangible to educators, parents, and students.

Ironically, in contrast to my practice, Action Potential does not delve deep into learning challenges, disabilities, or social/emotional vulnerabilities. The intent is not one of ignorance or avoidance, but rather to first explore the foundations of optimal learning. The hope is that by providing this foundation, we can consider additional ways in which learning challenges can be better supported.

Additionally, I want to acknowledge there are aspects of this book that are intentionally simplistic about learning. Like many educators and parents, I am far more invested in the health and happiness of children with a focus on how we, as a society, can do better to nurture inclusive, kind, and engaged global citizens. Children need to feel safe, cared for, and loved by adults. However, I also find that much of that ambition and wish presupposes that certain important competencies have been developed which help children engage in those endeavors.

Ultimately, *Action Potential* aims to provide direct answers regarding the neurocognitive and psychological characteristics that enrich a child's learning capabilities. While growth mindset and grit have become popular constructs, executive functioning has yet to earn the same academic recognition. I find this not only illogical by our current understanding of learning, but a striking oversight given the historical and evolutionary impact executive functioning has had on human survival. Action Potential examines the power of executive functioning, growth minded thinking and grit as core components to successful learning. I not only discuss the importance of these competencies, but the timing of their development and their significance within an educational framework.

CHAPTER 1

Brain-based Learning: The Next Big Thing

Education has always been about the next big thing. Forever gone are the days when school primarily took the form of recitation literacy, with only well-to-do students sitting in rows memorizing facts and learning classical languages. Since then, education has seen the emergence of numerous trends and programs, all driven by the same underlying goals: *How can we better understand children?* and *What is the optimal way to help them learn?* Effective teaching methods have traditionally been informed by advancements in our understanding of child development or related philosophies of learning and enrichment. What most of these methods have in common is their focus on *styles of learning* and/or developing environments *tailored to specific learning approaches.*

In more recent years, brain-based learning—as if there was any other kind!—has garnered significant attention in providing a road map to optimal learning, albeit one that has not yet been well defined. More specifically, focus has been directed toward the neurosciences to help uncover how we can maximize the potential of children at various developmental stages.

Many of the pedagogical tools and philosophies upon which schools are based look to what we know (or knew) about child development and what those founders believed as the ultimate goals of education. Some of these are highly recognizable, successful models in school programs across the world. For example, Montessori schools provide progressive approaches to learning that aim to foster individual expression and exploration as well as self-paced learning. Other well known models provide structure and sequence without the rigid reliance on traditional reference materials (Waldorf/Steiner schools), or use project-based approaches to investigate and document learning (Reggio Emilia). Likewise, play-based (versus teacher-directed) preschool programs have recently sprouted. Backed by empirical evidence, these programs emphasize the importance of play in the development of social skills and enriched cognitive functioning.

Beyond the early education framework, simple applications such as the Socratic method of learning have become commonplace. This method is based on inquiry and discussion that fosters critical thinking and higher understanding. Across the core subjects of reading, writing, and math, the market is awash with programs and products to foster the development of these skills. These approaches have been advanced partially by social policy, including the very notion of public schooling as a mandatory, government-funded endeavor driven by the understanding that society benefits from the education of all children. Similarly, the Head Start program was developed under President Lyndon B. Johnson in the 1960s to combat generational poverty by providing additional resources to low-income children and their families. Like education, the pursuit of new ways of teaching is propelled by a constant search for the next best thing; the truth is, we are desperate to understand and master optimal academic performance. We want not only to help our children keep up, but also find the magical formula to help teach our children how to succeed. In a now firmly established era of instant information and emerging technology with the potential to revolutionize all aspects of daily life, the pressure is stronger than ever to find the best methods of how we can learn, do, and achieve faster, better, and longer.

Brain-Based Learning and Education

Research in neuroscience and learning has made significant, dramatic developments over the last few decades, investigating new ways to bridge the gap between the two domains. In the past twenty years, the field of brain-based education has blossomed as an independent discipline solely focused on connecting what we know about the brain to educational programming and policy. In the last decade, the foundation of the International Mind and Brain Education Society was established. IMBE seeks "to facilitate cross-cultural collaboration in all fields that are relevant to connecting mind, brain, and education in research, theory, and/or practice." Taking their goals a step further, IMBE developed a peer-reviewed journal in 2007 (Mind, Brain, and Education). More recently, SAGE Publishing, one of the leading publishers of academic journals, announced a new journal, Educational Neuroscience, in 2015.

Academia has also come to realize the profound importance of brain-based education. Columbia University Teachers College's master's program in neuroscience and education touts its degree as the first offered that "focus(es) on the educational and clinical implications of recent advances in understanding brain-behavior relationships." Harvard University and the University of Texas at Arlington are among several institutions offering advanced degrees in "Mind, Brain, and Education.' Moreover, during his presidency, Barack Obama launched the $3 billion BRAIN (**B**rain **R**esearch through **A**dvancing **I**nnovative **N**eurotechnologies) Initiative, partially to "deepen our understanding of how we think, learn, and remember." The initiative, still in its early stages, has set out to unlock the mysteries of the brain through groundbreaking projects such as mapping chemical activity and neural circuits in the brain to identify the networks responsible for cognitive, emotional, and behavioral activities.

The interest, funding, and evidence for brain-based education is increasing; however, in terms of how these developments have entered the classroom, we are still far behind understanding the power of these findings and their applications. In other words, we are not yet uniformly using what we know about the brain and early development to establish new pedagogical methods. The reason is not hard to intuit; the divide between the lab and the classroom can be a bridge very difficult to traverse. Researchers do not conduct their work in a classroom, and teachers do not work in a lab. And while both educators and neuroscientists are equally interested in the same thing—how individuals learn—they tend to stay within their lanes, speaking what seems like two completely different languages, separated by discipline-specific jargon.

In the last ten to fifteen years, however, the divide has started to break down, as brain-based education has begun to infiltrate classrooms and provide the basis for school programming and curriculum development. Education has always embraced an evidence-based approach, and the evidence is stark—and mounting. It is time for educational policymakers and curriculum developers to reflect on what science has demonstrated about children's developing brains and bring those findings directly into the classroom.

Grit and Growth Mindset

So, how far have we come? What breakthroughs have there been in education, and does science back it up? Increasingly, theories have begun to emerge, and so too has peer-reviewed evidence to substantiate the claims. In fact, of the wave of recent educational trends and think-pieces (much of which fails to rise beyond the fodder of pop psychology), two pivotal theories both rooted in lab-driven human behavioral research, have recently emerged and quickly gained momentum among educators and parents. These concepts have been able to do so by tackling a slightly different question, not one of *doing* but of *feeling*: what should we teach our children to *feel* when faced with the challenge of learning? What are the psychological factors—the attitudes and beliefs—that we should instill in our children that will help them succeed?

To answer these questions, researchers have examined classroom behavior and student attitudes to discover who the best learners were and what character traits they tended to have in common. The two concepts emerging from this line of inquiry are simple but significant and have swept education by storm: the first being **grit**, the brainchild of Angela Duckworth, professor of psychology at the University of Pennsyl-Pennsylvania and the Founder and CEO of Character Lab. The second concept is **growth mindset**, introduced by world-renowned Stanford University psychologist, Carol Dweck.

In answering how successful students attain that success, Dweck found, in both observational and experimental research, that those students viewed failure not as a limit, but as an opportunity for growth (i.e., what Dweck terms a "growth mindset"). Those who went beyond easy, effortless successes to persist to reach goals despite challenges reaped the most academic rewards. That is, they had what Duckworth terms "grit."

"Well, duh," a cynic might say. "If you work hard and don't give up at the first challenge, of course you'll succeed!"

But what Dweck and Duckworth have demonstrated convincingly is that these ideas are not just platitudes on a poster, but individual psychological constructs that can be actively fostered within the classroom. They also showed that doing so creates learners at a distinct advantage in their ability, capacity, and interest to learn.

The concepts of grit and growth mindset stand apart from prior trends and more traditional educational methods by identifying specific traits within students that relate directly to their ability to learn. In other words, they propose a radical notion: to create the right kinds of environments for student success, one must first build the right kinds of students. The appeal of this is clear: these are characteristics—or rather, "character skills"—that all students can build at any point in their academic careers. In addition, these results are easily applicable to and visible in a wide range of environments, be they academic, social, or professional. Most relevant in terms of bridging the gap between the world of research and the world of education, growth mindset and grit are the closest education has yet come to embracing new approaches based on well-researched psychological constructs.

Grit and growth mindset are new approaches to optimizing academic development and describe two fundamental building blocks for a student's success. However, while focusing on psychological factors and character traits, the discussion has again veered away from brain-based education—further confirming the gap that still exists. There is no question that perseverance, resilience, and determination are essential characteristics for successful learning. Moreover, having the insight to see that learning is about the process more than performance is critical to orientating children to the work of learning. But what groundwork must be laid for a child's developing brain to acquire these skills? At what point is the developing brain most amenable to these interventions? The answer that this book advances is that, to understand and optimize how one learns in the classroom, we must understand and optimize learning in the brain.

The Brain and Its Executive

The human brain is made of a complex neural network not often fully understood or appreciated. We take for granted that every thought we have, every emotion we feel, all the movements our body makes, and our awareness of the world are the result of our wondrous brain. Your ability to read these words is only possible because there are over a hundred billion neurons instantly messaging each other. No artificial network can even compare to what the human brain does every nanosecond of every day of its living existence. To understand the mechanisms that make us learners, we first should have a basic understanding of the brain itself.

Within that complex neural network, the brain's **executive functioning system** holds the key to unlocking optimal learning and overall functioning. Often the analogy of a leader or CEO is used to describe executive functioning, as someone who decides a course of action, issues commands, and ensures that the commands are carried out. In the same way, the intricate neural network that carries out these executive functions has the power to put plans, actions, or ideas into effect. Specifically, our executive functioning skills govern our ability to productively orchestrate several types of skills, allowing us to concentrate on multiple streams of information simultaneously, screen for errors, revise plans in light of new information, and manage self-control.

In early development, emergent executive functioning skills help young children remember steps in performing arithmetic, aid them as they learn to read and write, participate in class discussions, and engage in sustained play with other children. Developing proficient executive functioning skills in childhood and adolescence provides the foundation required for success in academic, social, and everyday life.

This is not new information. We know that a strong foundation of executive functioning skills is associated with long-term (lifelong) positive outcomes. In fact, New Zealand has been ahead of the game in studying executive functioning skills since 1972. The Dunedin Multidisciplinary Health and Development Research Unit (DMHDRU) followed the development of one thousand children since 1972 (with a 96 percent retention rate). They found that the children with the most self-control experienced the most positive life outcomes, across many measures of well-being: physical health, alcohol and drug dependence, personal finances, and court convictions.

In 1982, Muriel Lezak, a contemporary American neuropsychologist, wrote that the executive functions of the frontal lobes are "the heart of all socially useful, personally enhancing, constructive, and creative abilities. Impairment or loss of these functions compromises a person's capacity to maintain an independent, constructively self-serving, and socially productive life no matter how well he can see and hear, walk and talk, and perform tests." That certainly puts in perspective just how important our executive function skills are to our functional existence.

Nature or Nurture

It is important to overstate that we are not born with executive functioning skills—we are born with the potential to develop them. The genes a child inherits do not determine his or her exact capabilities or skills, but they do supply a range of developmental outcomes. This range is maximized through the quality of interactions and experiences that parents, communities, and institutions provide for them. Developmentally, executive functioning skills begin to develop soon after a child is born, with dramatic growth observed during ages three to five. Development continues throughout adolescence and into early adulthood.

While all is not lost if ideal environments are not created in the early years of childhood—in other words, the brain has the neural plasticity to continually develop skills—it is much easier to cement this skill set at an early age. As the authors of Welcome to Your Child's Brain have said, "You can change the floor plan of your house after it is complete, but it is much easier to change it during construction."

CHAPTER 2
Prehistory and Your Brain

While educational trends have come and gone, arriving at a scientific understanding about the nature and importance of executive functioning has slowly come into focus over the last two centuries. Throughout that span, science has labored to discover that what initially was considered an unimportant, dormant aspect of the brain is, in fact, the foundation and backbone of our individual day-to-day functioning. This is so true that archaeologists and psychologists have argued that, evolutionarily speaking, the abilities associated with executive functioning were the key acquisition responsible for the development of modern, evolutionarily advanced thinking.

The Human Skull and Vertical Space

In the fossil record, the transformation from the early humans to modern-day *Homo sapiens* is a story that can be told most simply in the silhouette of the skull. At the core of that story is the evolution of the human brain and the growth of the frontal lobes. This part of the brain, home to the network of neurons that comprise the executive functioning system, plays a pivotal role not just in the success and optimal functioning of modern individuals, but on a broader level provided the crucial steps forward in modern thinking that ensured the very survival of the human species. Understanding the evolution of the human brain also provides historical weight and clarity to the role that executive functioning plays in carrying out the seemingly simple, yet complex cognitive activities without which learning and adaptation would be impossible.

Across a span of two million years, the size of the human brain tripled both in size and in weight, growing from a little over one pound to about three. This increase in mass was, more importantly, accompanied by considerable growth in the quantity and intricacies of the connections within the brain, particularly around the frontmost part of the brain, which saw the greatest amount of changes in size and sophistication.

Comparing the skulls of *Homo erectus* (older species) and Homo sapiens, the dramatic difference lies in not only the size, but also in the shape of the skulls. The growth of the frontmost part of the brain was so significant that housing this bigger, better-connected brain involved the restructuring of the skull itself into a thin-walled, high-vaulted dome with a vertical wall for the forehead. This physio-structural change reflected the neurostructural changes taking place inside of it; the matter of the brain inside of the newly fashioned skull also evolved, developing a neocortex (literally, "new bark" in Latin) with distinct, specialized frontal lobes.

Frontal Lobes—The Ultimate Networker

In terms of size, there is some dispute regarding whether humans possess larger frontal lobes compared to our most closely related primate cousins. However, what sets humans apart is the *organization* of our frontal lobes. Greater connectivity exists from the frontal lobe to other brain structures compared to other primates (and non-primates), which allows better abilities to process and integrate large volumes of information as well as organize that information for future action.

The frontal lobe's extensive network of connections includes areas of the brain responsible for short- and long-term memory, emotion, sensory integration, the regulation of movement, motivation, language processing, etc. This evolutionary shift in human physiology and neurobiology occurred in tandem with the evolution of modern thought—that is, the shift away from a primitive brain, driven by impulses and basic instincts to survive, including the drive for food, sex, and the fight/flight/freeze reaction to danger.

The "new bark" of the brain, particularly the expansion in size and complexity in the foremost area, allowed more sophisticated thought to take place. With the forehead came control over instincts and the facilitation of adaptable behaviors, such as conscious planning, reasoning,

HUMAN FRONTAL LOBE EVOLUTION

oThe high, straight forehead that characterizes modern humans, superseding the prominent brow ridges of our ancestors, is due to the expansion of the cortex, and especially the prefrontal cortex, in our species.

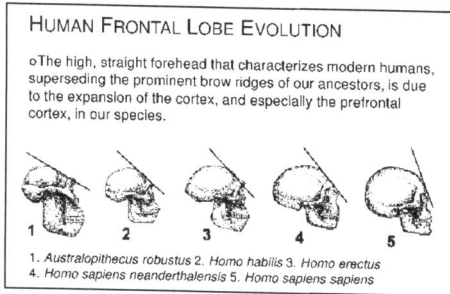

1. *Australopithecus robustus* 2. *Homo habilis* 3. *Homo erectus* 4. *Homo sapiens neanderthalensis* 5. *Homo sapiens sapiens*

logical thinking, and language. With it came the advanced development of tools, the emergence of symbolic art, and complex social rituals. The sophistication in the human brain's functioning permitted a greater range of thought, judgment, and reasoning. This was an evolution critical not only in increasing our survivability as a species, but also in distancing humans from lower-order animals, which only apply instinct to their behavioral decisions.

Control Thyself

The field of paleoanthropology, which studies the stages of progression in human development, widely regards the evolution of the foremost part of the brain as a pivotal juncture in the emergence of modern thought. Specifically, this was driven by advancements in the acquisition of certain types of cognitive skills, which are responsible for making judgments, reasoning, and weighing outcomes, social communication, and self control—a critical guard against our sometimes-unreliable instincts.

Self-control is particularly important to highlight, as it is in many ways the measuring stick of being human. It is not a coincidence that, when we encounter individuals who lack self-control or self-discipline, we describe them as "animal-like" or "child-like," that is, like beings that lack intellect and reasoning ability and are instead driven by their primitive instincts. In contrast, our fascination with sophisticated animals, such as dolphins, chimpanzees, squid, and octopi, results from how "human-like" they can behave because of their self-regulated behavior. This control over our behaviors, apart from a reliance solely on instinct, was the key aspect of human evolution that increased reproductive fitness and, in turn, the overall survivability of our species. The dramatic advance in mental complexity compared to the more primitive "lizard brain" (a term referring to the evolutionarily oldest part of the brain) is shown by the name that we selected for ourselves, Homo sapiens, meaning "wise human." The wisdom, of course, refers not only to our brain's capacity to store large amounts of information, but also our ability to actually do something with that information. For that, we have our foreheads to thank. By "foreheads," what we mean is the part of the brain that sits just on the other side of the skull. It is the frontal lobes that are responsible for modern human thought. But how?

The Frontal Lobe and Its Core Functions

The various processes of executive functioning (including but not limited to problem solving, inhibition, working memory, planning, reasoning, and goal setting) are governed by the frontal lobe, which is also responsible for motor functions and the regulation of attention. It is hard to overstate the core functions of the frontal lobe, which is crucial to many of the most advanced human behaviors. A healthy, well-functioning frontal lobe is what enables the successful completion of tasks, from the most complex projects to tasks as basic and quotidian as figuring out what to wear in the morning. For example, the frontal lobe lets an individual create a mental representation of his or her wardrobe, plan based on the day's activities, decide what to put on, as well as organize muscles to perform the motoric task of dressing oneself. The frontal lobe is, most plainly, the seat of reasoned mental activity and reactivity; it takes in information and synthesizes that knowledge to form plans and beliefs, as well as regulate emotions, behaviors, and attention.

It may seem outrageous that one of the most important components of the brain has historically been so poorly understood. Researchers in neuroscience and its related fields (neurobiology, anatomy, neuropsychology, etc.) are only just now beginning to fully understand this area of the brain and the executive functions wired within. How is that so? The short answer is that the remarkable complexity of the frontal lobes and vast, diverse range of governance of executive functioning over actions and behaviors made it difficult to even ask the right questions, let alone uncover the right answers.

CHAPTER 3
History of the Frontal Lobes

Our current understanding of the complex role played by the frontal lobe is typically traced to early work by clinicians in the mid to late 19th century. As tools to access and study the brain were quite limited (there was no such thing as an MRI at the time), much of the scientific understanding of the brain and its functions came from observing what happened when certain areas became damaged, either during brain surgery or post-mortem analyses of patients with known head traumas.

Phineas Gage

One of the earliest and most well-known documented cases, familiar to any first-year psychology student, is the story of Phineas Gage, a 25-year-old foreman of little repute until a freak accident turned him into neuroscience's most famous patient. On September 13, 1848, while attempting to clear a path for a new railroad, Gage was caught in a sudden explosion that propelled a three-and-a-half-foot tamping iron (referred to quite sensationally in subsequent literature as a "crowbar") through his left eye and out the top of his head.

The massive brain injury destroyed large parts of Gage's frontal lobe—yet, remarkably, he *survived*. More amazingly, he was walking and talking within minutes, conscious and capable of relating to his surroundings and medical team.

The town doctor who attended to the injury, Dr. John Martyn Harlow, described the case as "unparalleled" and "truly terrific." However, the impact of the damage to the frontal lobe became apparent over time, as remarked upon by Dr. Harlow, who followed Gage's case until Gage's death in 1861. Harlow's follow-up report in 1868, twenty years after the initial incident, noted that while the injury healed well and Gage retained full physical functioning and intellectual faculties, he experienced a personality change so severe that he became unrecognizable to those who knew him best.

Gage's injury, which obliterated his left frontal lobe and likely damaged parts of his right frontal lobe, resulted in the loss of the faculties controlled by that area of the brain: he struggled to plan effectively, regulate his emotions, sustain attention, and control his instincts and impulses. Perhaps most telling is the description of Gage's demeanor as "childlike," striking upon an understanding of frontal lobe development (and its role in self-regulatory behaviors) that would not arrive in scientific literature for another 100 years.

Science and the Frontal Lobe Conundrum

As noted in Gage's case, these changes were described as shifts in personality and/or alterations of character, alluding to early researchers' difficulties in identifying clear-cut terminology to describe the functions of this area of the brain. World War I and the multitude of veterans returning from the front lines with brain injuries and traumas created further opportunities for physicians to learn more about the brain's localized functions. Through the next few decades, functions such as flexibility/perseverative behavior, organization, and sequencing, as well as abstract thought and problem solving were added to the ever-growing list of abilities adversely affected by insults to the frontal lobe. The unrelated nature of these skills created a conundrum for scientists who were grappling with the specific functions of the frontal lobe.

Throughout the early and middle parts of the twentieth century, debate continued over the exact nature and precise functions of the prefrontal area in day-to-day functioning, particularly because of the multitude of processes disrupted (typically varying widely between patients) and the difficulty in placing these functions under the umbrella of a single cognitive network. As a result, the functions of the frontal lobe continued to emerge as an increasing area of interest for neurologists, anatomists, and other clinicians, fueled by larger developments in the mapping of specific parts of the brain. Slowly, with the understanding brought about by clearer maps of the brain's architecture, the picture of executive functioning (though not yet referred to by the term) came into focus. While work continued on human and animal patients with frontal lobe injuries and lesions, the first half of the twentieth century featured a pivot toward experimental research on healthy, otherwise normally functioning subjects.

Alexander Luria and His
Explanation of the Network

Without question, one of the most important researchers that advanced our understanding of the front lobe was Alexander R. Luria, a Soviet psychologist. Luria proposed that the frontal lobe was critical in planning, organization, behavior regulation, and processing and sorting relevant information from the environment. The frontal lobe, he theorized, "*synthesizes information about the outside world and is the means whereby the behavior of an organism is regulated in conformity with the effect produced by its actions.*" Without this underlying system, "*goal-directed, selective behavior is impossible.*"

Luria and other contemporary research yielded many descriptions of similar phenomena, although there was little in the way of common terminology. In fact, many of the most well-known developmental (child) psychologists were also making significant advancements in what we now know about executive functioning, specifically relating to impulse control and self-regulation, planning, and flexibly integrating information while learning and engaging in day to day tasks.

The work of Jean Piaget is perhaps the most well known, alongside that of Lev Vygotsky, whose theories were further fleshed out and explored by Alexander Luria. Although their approaches and developmental models varied widely, the takeaway is that developmental psychology as a field began to explore the underlying process of planning, learning, and abstract thinking. Again, the term "executive functioning" had yet to come into play—although across disciplines, the research in the development, deployment, and (in some instances) degeneration of these higher-level functions was well under way.

A Silly Sentence and a New Scientific Term

So, what to call this system of connected cognitive abilities forming the basis of all complex mental activity and without which individuals were prone to impulsive, inappropriate, and unregulated responses? Credit for the term **executive functioning** is most often attributed to Karl Pribram, who in 1973 first used the term "executive" to describe the role played by the frontal lobe in decision making and information processing. He fleshed out the term further in a 1976 article, which includes the following exchange with Dominick Purpura, a fellow neuroscientist:

> *PURPURA: I am going to give a silly sentence. When I leave a blank you answer it. I, Karl Pribram, believe that the role of the frontal lobe is to...*
>
> *PRIBRAM: ...act as an executor to the rest of the brain. It sets up a programme or a context in which all the other activity takes place. A programme that has all the executive functions of the brain.*

CHAPTER 4

Executive Functioning: A Definition, Please?

The human brain has evolved to develop executive functioning via its frontal lobes, but we struggle to understand and define what those functions are and how they interact with each other as well as other parts of the brain. There are both intimidating and voluminous references, books, and articles that discuss executive functioning, from what it is to what it does and how it develops. Moreover, there are countless books that describe what happens when there is a breakdown in executive functioning. Part of the confusion surrounding the term "executive functioning" lies in the fact that the term refers to both a singular system as well as the multiple, interdependent elements that comprise that system. This means that "executive functioning" can be defined as a set of skills, or it can be used to describe the overall functionality of those elements working in unison. It can also be discussed at the level of neuroarchitecture and neural systems, or at the behavioral and functional level. Incredibly, more than 30 unique definitions exist to explain the executive functioning construct. If that's not enough, the increasing interest in executive functions that exploded (so to speak) in the 2000s has thus far yielded over 8,500 academic articles, books, and dissertations written during the last fifteen years alone.

What Is Executive Functioning, and Why Can't We All Agree?

Most experts agree that executive functioning describes a set of cognitive abilities that control and regulate *other* abilities and behaviors. For example, executive functions control one's ability to start and stop actions, to monitor and change behavior as needed, and to plan future behavior when faced with novel tasks and situations. Executive functions give our brains the ability to anticipate outcomes and adapt to changing situations. More specifically, to deliberately solve a problem, one needs to do several smaller things in a specific sequence: identify what needs to be accomplished, devise a plan to accomplish said task, carry out that plan, and evaluate the success of the attempted solution.

There are several common and useful analogies deployed to describe executive functioning as a system and its constituent parts, such as an air traffic control system or a leader/CEO. The former is a useful analogy that depicts a colorful image of executive functioning as an air traffic controller that manages multiple schedules, arrivals, departures, and runways, day in and day out; the latter reflects a hierarchical system in which executive functioning works to devise a specific plan or direction, organize subordinates toward fulfilling that goal, and see the project through.

These analogies, while colorful, do not give a definition that we can effectively use within our neuro-scientific or educational nomenclature. The fact is that the complexity and multifunctional abilities of executive functioning make it hard to pin down. This is because it is not only a combination of specific subregions of the brain (within the frontal lobe and particularly the prefrontal cortex) but also the interconnectivity and communication of complex networks in our brains. Essentially, the problem that experts encounter is developing a consensus of what specific functions make up the set of these proverbial CEO or air traffic control abilities, some of which are concrete and easily understood and others that are nuanced and less tangible.

Executive Functioning and Its Core

While there are multiple definitions of "executive functioning," there are core elements of consensus for researchers and experts. These core executive functions, which are thought to underlie all planning, problem solving, reasoning, and learning include: **working memory, self-control** and **mental flexibility**. Working memory is the ability to mentally hold and retrieve information. Self-control is the ability to resist several thoughts or actions to focus on one. Mental flexibility is the ability to consider multiple ideas and see different perspectives. The combination of these skills allows us to focus, hold onto, and work with information in our minds while filtering distractions and switching gears.

It may seem surprising to distill executive functioning to these core components. But the truth is, while many sources define "executive functions" as a laundry list of skills associated with higher-level thinking, decision making, and project management, every single one of those functions is directly reliant upon working memory, self-control, and/or mental flexibility.

CHAPTER 5
Working Memory

Working memory is the temporary sticky note in our brain. It can be thought of as a *mental work space* or mental drafting table where information is held and manipulated for some immediate purpose. That *purpose* is to hold new information in place so our brain can briefly work with that information and connect it to other relevant information. Working memory should not be underestimated, as this neural sticky note is quite possibly the single most important cognitive skill within our brain. It is significant, if not imperative, to everyday thinking, doing, and being.

In the context of evolution, working memory has been brought to center stage as the essential, if not pivotal, variable to modern thought. While most would attribute the acquisition of language and the ability to think symbolically as the most distinguishing evolutionary features of modern thought, it is actually working memory that has garnered the most attention. Veritably, the development of language and/or the ability to create symbolic representations is the result of our working memory. Our very survival relied on the development of our working memory so we could successfully engage in problem solving and long-range planning. This very notion became the sole focus of the book *The Rise of Homo Sapiens: The Evolution of Human Thinking*. Based on archaeological evidence, the authors theorized that the biological change in cognition, namely, working memory, explained the emergence of modern humans.

Working Memory – Leader of the Pack

Make no mistake, as our understanding of the human brain grows, working memory will continue to emerge as an important, if not the most important, cognitive function for human development. Our working memories are a powerful tool that extends beyond simply allowing the brain to engage in daily functioning. The versatility, yet delicate nature, of working memory can be described in many ways.

In a simple example, Bluma Zeigarnik, a Soviet psychologist, noticed that waiters employed specific, efficient use of working memory on the job. Zeigarnik observed a waiter who could remember a seemingly endless number of items that had been ordered by his customers. However, once the food was delivered and the bill paid, he no longer recalled what he

Short-term vs. Working Memory

Short-term memory and working memory are not the same, though the two concepts are very much related. "Short-term memory" is the *holding* of information, while "working memory" is a more complex system, that not only holds information (in short-term memory), but also employs other processing mechanisms to use the information being held. Thus, working memory incorporates both temporary storage (short-term memory) and the concurrent processing of that *held* information.

had just served. His working memory operated remarkably efficiently—essentially, this waiter's mental drafting table was cleared of unnecessary information to provide room for new, incoming information (i.e., new food orders).

A more common example of working memory is mental arithmetic. Imagine, for example, trying to multiply 34 and 37 without the use of pen and paper or calculator. First you would need to hold the two numbers in your working memory. The next step would be to use learned multiplication rules to calculate the products of successive pairs of numbers, adding the new products to your working memory as you go. Finally, you would need to add together the products held in working memory, (hopefully) resulting in the correct answer. Without working memory, this kind of complex mental activity would be impossible. We could not keep in mind salient information while processing other relevant material.

With the above *in* mind, it is not surprising that one's working memory capacity correlates with a wide variety of critical cognitive abilities, including reading comprehension, vocabulary learning, language comprehension, language acquisition, second language learning, spelling, storytelling, etc. It pervades our daily existence, from helping children remember the rules of a game as they're playing it to helping an adult remember her to do list for the day. Over one's lifespan, a person's working memory capacity grows in both the amount of information that can be held without loss and the duration for which it can be held.

Working Memory – Delicate and Fragile

While working memory is a useful, flexible system crucial to humans for everyday functioning, it is remarkably sensitive and fragile. It requires continuous mental engagement (i.e., effort), is prone to errors, and is limited in capacity. The size and processing power of working memory differs from person to person, but even a well-oiled, high-capacity, efficient working memory can run into problems because of working memory's unique vulnerability to distraction and, in turn, information loss.

Even minor distractions such as a passing, but unrelated thought, can interrupt and wipe information from the drafting table. And once that information is gone, it is irretrievable. For information to be recalled—say, a phone number—it must first be encoded and stored. However, because the information in working memory is often very recently obtained and still "in play," so to speak, the encoding process is vulnerable to interruption. In the case of the phone number, a person may remember the last few numbers at the expense of earlier digits. For this reason, there are many tools and strategies people employ—often unconsciously—to sustain information in their minds and protect it from catastrophic loss.

CHAPTER 6
Self-Control

Ultimately, when we're talking about self-control, what that means is self-regulation in service of a greater goal: being able to self-monitor impulses and emotions, and purposefully determine whether acting on them is appropriate, given the circumstances. Self-control is the ability to restrain and self-regulate purposefully and consciously, thus allowing us to behave in a measured manner.

Evolutionarily speaking, the increase in humans' capacity for self-control was one of the primary developmental advancements that increased the long-term survivability of our species. Once humans learned to control the fight-or-flight impulse and could better engage in problem-solving behavior, that is, purposefully think through stressful or challenging situations in a more measured and reasoned way, our longevity as a species increased.

Self-control means being able to stop an action or plan that is already in motion (a sort of behavioral inertia) the moment a change occurs in the environment that renders the action inappropriate or sub-optimal.

At a basic level, think of the game Simon Says, in which the task of inhibiting a response is central to winning or, at least, staying in the game. Functionally, it means staying focused on your work by overriding impulses to check emails, instantly replying to text messages, or checking how many likes you received on a social media post. It is thinking before we act, and perhaps biting our tongues before saying something we'll regret.

Terminology Confusion: Self Control, or...?

Experts love to invent their own terms and phrases, with what seems like only a shade of difference between them. "Self-control" in clinical terms has appeared as inhibitory control, self-regulation, effortful control, etc. All these terms describe slight differences or various aspects of the same construct (i.e., self-control). For example, "self-regulation" focuses on emotional control. "Inhibitory control" is specific to cognitive control, sans emotion. "Effortful control" is described as a temperament. Respecting the differentiation is important and valid. However, for the purpose of this book, the focus is on distilling key characteristics in learning and development which integrate the aforementioned terms: self-control.

Our brains need to exercise self-control to survive; it's needed to sustain focus, learn information, and remain clear-headed enough to process and reason through options. Most often, success comes down to choosing the pain of discipline over the ease of distraction. The term for this is **delayed gratification**, that is, putting off a desired, short-term reward for longer-term gain. Not surprisingly, the willingness to delay gratification is a strong proxy measure of an individual's self-control.

This measure is so strong that you only need a single marshmallow to prove it. This may seem like a non sequitur, but a famous experiment conducted several decades ago empirically captured the relationship between self-control and delayed gratification in a way that has made marshmallows synonymous with these terms.

Cue the Marshmallow Man

In the late 1960s and early 1970s, Walter Mischel started a series of studies to examine self-control and delayed gratification in children. These children were assessed regarding both if and how they could contain their immediate impulses to achieve a greater reward. The experiment began in a preschool where four- and five-year-old children were brought into a private room and seated at a table where a very tempting marshmallow was placed in front of them. The researcher told the child that he would leave the room and that, if the child did not eat the marshmallow while he was away, he or she would be rewarded with a second marshmallow. However, if the child decided to eat the first one before the researcher came back, the child would not get a second treat.

The choice was simple: get one marshmallow right now or two later. The researcher then left the room for fifteen minutes. The reactions of some of the children, whose behavior was recorded during the waiting period, were quite comical. As one would expect, some kids immediately ate the first marshmallow. Others engaged in various antics to avoid temptation: they bounced, squirmed, and scooted in their chairs to restrain themselves, but many eventually gave in to temptation only a few minutes later. However, a few of the children were able to wait the entire fifteen minutes and receive their double reward. But the experiment did not end there; the researchers kept track of these children and followed them for forty years. What they found was interesting.

The children who waited for the larger reward were consistently more successful students and adults in later life. These kids showed better executive functioning skills, particularly self-control; relatedly, they showed a better ability to cope with stress and frustration. They also showed better ability to focus and persist compared to their non-delaying peers.

What's important to highlight is that these "delayers" *were not necessarily the smartest kids in the group.* They simply had the best self-control. Additionally, the children

Caveat of the Marshmallow Test

So, why not just do away with standardized testing and give all children the marshmallow test? Why isn't it commonplace at pediatrician visits, alongside vaccines, flu shots, and hearing and vision tests? Like all experiments, this famous study should be interpreted in its specific context. It provided one piece of data, and we know that humans (and especially child development) are extraordinarily complex. Thus, narrowing down the success and potential of any child to ninety calories of spongy sugar has been assailed as naive and far too simplistic—and rightfully so! There have been numerous criticisms regarding the validity of the study, with many citing sample sizes as too small and homogenous to support sweeping generalizations. Other critics have argued that the marshmallow test actually measures trust in authority more than the willingness to delay gratification. Despite these criticisms, the implications of the study related to the delay of gratification and self-control should not get thrown out. No one can deny that self-control is critical to success.

who successfully waited to receive the second marshmallow performed better on standardized tests, achieved higher SAT scores, and showed lower levels of substance abuse, a lower likelihood of obesity, better responses to stress, better social skills as reported by their parents, and generally better scores on a range of other life measures.

While this study has had many implications, the role of self-control in the acquisition of academic skills has been an important finding corroborated by further studies that show its significant correlation with math and reading development.

New Zealand and the Dunedin Study

The infamous marshmallow test has attracted its fair share of attention, praise, and criticism over the years; however, a lesser-known albeit even more impressive study undertaken in New Zealand lends further credence to the idea that self-control is a fundamental aspect of development that is wide reaching and has lifelong implications. The study was created to better understand key aspects of child development and what variables organically and/or externally have significant long-term impacts.

To that end, the Dunedin Multidisciplinary Health and Development Study began tracking just over a thousand children who were born in the same city in the same year for an astounding forty-four years—and counting! The researchers have been following these individuals with minimal attrition (96 percent retention as of a 2012 paper). The Dunedin study, which has produced thousands of academic papers, has supplied valuable information about self-control and lifelong success. Of the one thousand children who were followed, those who at ages three to eleven were assessed to have the best self-control were more likely to become functional, low-risk teenagers. These kids were better at waiting their turn, less distracted, more persistent, and less impulsive. Moreover, they grew up to be adults with better physical and mental health, and better financial success. They also, in turn, used fewer societal resources, including reduced health care usage, fewer run-ins with the law, and less reliance on welfare.

Beyond Marshmallows

As compelling as the research has been, in isolation (as with the marshmallow experiment) and in longitudinal context (the Dunedin study), it is important to pause here and remind ourselves that humans are extremely complex and that the determinants of health and success are multifaceted and variable. Drawing a firm line from one data point to a separate outcome should be done sparingly, with caution and statistical rigor. However, none of those points should take away from the clear relationship that these two (and others, not recounted here) studies outline between self-control and lifelong success. Self-control is fundamental to remaining disciplined to achieve a given end.

CHAPTER 7
Mental Flexibility

The third core component in the schematic of executive functioning is mental flexibility. The more clinical term, which emphasizes the neurological basis of this ability, is "cognitive flexibility." Regardless of which term you use (this book will favor "mental flexibility"), what is being described is the brain's ability to adapt, mentally transition, and take on alternative perspectives. To put it another way, a person's mental flexibility (or lack thereof) reflects their neurological stubbornness, that is, whether that person can let go of an idea, action, or perspective, should a situation require it. Essentially, it is our ability to change our minds to adapt to changes in the environment, allowing us to see situations from another perspective and to incorporate or seek new information when one approach is no longer viable. Functionally, mental flexibility is broken into two mutually dependent and connected skills: flexible thinking and set shifting.

Flexible thinking refers to the ability to activate the mental pathways that make it possible for us to recognize a new element or perspective. In other words, flexible thinking allows us to think about something in a new way, be it a problem we are trying to solve or a statement or belief that we are trying to make sense of. Once the activation occurs, the next step is to make the mental shift to executing or focusing on those new, better solutions or options. Set shifting is what allows us to let go of the old way of thinking to use the new way. It is the ability to shift perspectives, that is, to deactivate the earlier perspective and import/load the different, more effective perspective.

Puzzle Time

Many puzzles and riddles play on the brain's ability to engage both aspects of mental flexibility, often presenting an obvious approach that turns out to be misleading. This then requires flexible thinking to find new ways of approaching the riddle and set shifting to reconsider the riddle using that approach. Consider the following sequence: what number fits in place of the question mark?

16 06 68 88 ? 98

When seeing numbers in sequence, many people's first impulse is to use math to determine the relationship between the numbers using some mathematical rule, for example, adding, subtracting, or multiplying some number to get the next number in the sequence. Once that fails, a flexible thinker may find a new strategy and consider each number not simply as one value, but as a combination of its individual digits. The prior, simpler strategy is deactivated, and this savvier puzzle solver activates a strategy of adding the digits of each number and hoping to see some pattern there. Unfortunately, there is none. The answer instead lies in a neat piece of flexible thinking, which involves one simple shift—*turning the piece of paper upside down.* Try it! The answer should become obvious.

When moving between ideas and perspectives, the simultaneous activation and deactivation that our brains must engage in is paramount to our ability to adapt and learn. Puzzles and riddles aside, the cognitive process that underlies mental flexibility is an incredibly complex one that involves the ability to address and interpret a new situation while restructuring prior knowledge to adapt to and assimilate new information.

If it sounds like we are wading back into the territory of working memory and self-control, that's because we are.

Creativity and cognitive flexibility go hand in hand. Having mental flexibility allows more creative thinking: generating novel approaches, seeing outside of convention, and finding ways to rework traditional ideas into new patterns. Artistic creativity is still not fully understood, and there remains very little consensus in neuroscience and psychology on what cognitive mechanisms are involved in creative acts (if only we could go back in time and stick Michelangelo in an MRI while he was painting the ceiling of the Sistine Chapel!). But one thing we do understand is that cognitive flexibility is an essential bedrock component of creative insight. Psychometric measurements of creativity lean heavily on this. For example, classic tests require the thinking of novel uses for familiar objects. (Try it: How many uses can you imagine for a paper clip? You have two minutes.) Creative problem solving in the classroom or in the workplace requires this same brainstorming capacity, stepping outside the rigid confines of traditional methods or answers to produce novel, innovative ideas.

These other core abilities are employed together to enable the success of mental flexibility—an idea that we will return to very shortly.

Assimilation and Accommodation

Mental flexibility has been reconstituted in many disciplines, though it has been most thoroughly explored in developmental psychology, where mental flexibility is considered one of the most important milestones of a child's development. Jean Piaget, a pioneer and influential figure in developmental psychology, described the cognitive development of children as *"a progressive reorganization of mental processes as a result of biological maturation and environmental experience. Children construct an understanding of the world around them, then experience discrepancies between what they already know and what they discover in their environment."* Resolving these discrepancies, Piaget argues, leads to advancements in children's ability to understand and make sense of their world. In Piagetian theory, this process is deconstructed into sequential processes of **assimilation** and **accommodation**.

Assimilation is analogous to the aforementioned concept of flexible thinking, namely, the ability to activate the mental pathways that make it possible for, in this case, a child to recognize and deal with a new situation or perspective. It is an active process, which involves acknowledging the significance of a new piece of information which runs counter to a person's existing knowledge (or, for Piaget's specific context, a child's internal representation of the world). The next step is to *accommodate* the new piece of information by merging it with prior knowledge. In other words, shifting set: deactivating the prior perspective and expanding it to include and accommodate the new piece of information.

Disequilibrium and Theory of Mind

It may appear a seamless and obvious sequence, particularly for a fully developed and capable adult brain. However, the process from assimilation to accommodation, from thinking flexibly to shifting set, is inherently complex, even for adults. People of all ages struggle to tolerate dissonance, ambiguity, and/or outcomes that are contrary to expectation. Piaget explains it well as a state of disequilibrium. The brain does not do particularly well with items that do not make sense within an existing framework. The ability to think flexibly offers a path toward alleviating mental discomfort and restoring balance by shifting perspectives to include the new information or adapt to the new experience.

Piaget's model of assimilation and accommodation does not cite the terms "mental flexibility" or "executive functioning" by name. (Recall, these terms came into use much later in the psychology literature). Nevertheless, the construct he describes and the remarkable process by which the brain must constantly incorporate information and adapt to new stimuli perfectly captures the role of mental flexibility in learning and in life.

In this way, mental flexibility forms the cornerstone of social-emotional understanding. Being able to empathize with others and/or make any kind of social judgment requires shifting between multiple psychological perspectives, which may operate under different rules. That is, individuals possess varying desires, interests, beliefs, experiential backgrounds, culture norms and values, etc. All of these may diverge from yours in a given moment or situation. Flexibly shifting between one's own judgments and others is what helps us to navigate complex social situations successfully.

This notion, which developmental psychologists call the *theory of mind*, refers to the human assumption (or theory) that others also have minds—and those minds can work differently from our own. In short: *I think, therefore I am. I can see that you are, so I guess you must think, too.* This isn't something that humans are born with, though we have the innate capacity to develop it. This facet of mental flexibility develops in early childhood, as children begin to explore, take in, and learn about their world.

CHAPTER 8
Trifecta of Core Skills

Completing most tasks requires the harmonization of several types of executive function skills. At the core of this neural harmony are working memory, self-control, and cognitive flexibility. We know that in most real-life experiences, these three functions are not entirely exclusive but, rather, they work together to produce more competent executive functioning. And these core components give us the ability to access higher-level skills.

What separates these three components (working memory, self-regulation, and mental flexibility) is that they are the underpinning for all the other skills that fall under the "executive functioning" umbrella. Successful planning, for example, requires being able to hold a considerable amount of information in mind, mentally juggling these items, and determining the proper steps toward completion—all without losing information. Problem solving, likewise, requires the ability to flexibly shift through many options and outcomes, holding these future scenarios in mind to assess which provides the optimal solution. Ultimately, these core functions lay the groundwork for learning.

Executive Functioning Hierarchy:
Which Comes First?

So now that we've established the importance and necessity of these components, is there a clear hierarchy between these three functions? This is debatable, but many will argue it starts with working memory. Working memory is probably the single most important cognitive skill within our brains. It is significant, if not imperative, to everyday thinking, doing, and being. I think; therefore, I am. "To think" means to foster the active engagement of circulating information within our working memory, that is, the drafting table. Once information has been called to the neural drafting table, we need to impose some level of self-control to filter out distractions and/or unnecessary information.

As we will see in the upcoming chapters that review the development of each of these aspects, it also holds true that the emergence of mental flexibility depends on the development of working memory and self-control. To change perspectives, we need to inhibit (or deactivate) our earlier perspective and load into working memory (or activate) another perspective. It is in this sense that cognitive flexibility requires and builds on inhibitory control and working memory. For example, self-control skills measured at two years of age were found to predict abilities to successfully demonstrate theory of mind at age three. Similarly, for a student to successfully partake in a class discussion (i.e., generate a new perspective on the topic at hand), she must first be able to keep in mind relevant information about the material discussed as well as parse and evaluate salient points from her classmates' contributions. Once this information is laid out on the working memory/drafting table, the student must also work to resist (inhibit) internal and external distractions.

CHAPTER 9

The Learning Brain

Clearly, the core three domains of executive functions—working memory, self-control, and mental flexibility—are vital and evolutionarily critical faculties that, beyond merely ensuring our species' survival, laid the foundation for successful learning in the modern world. This is to say that executive functioning is the fundamental system that underlies all types of learning (academic, social) and developmental success. In the context of school and one's learning capacity, executive functioning has been described as the neurobiological foundation of academic development.

Thousands of books, dozens of theories, and many schools of thought have aimed to identify core aspects of early learning. However, these efforts do not uniformly adopt the development of executive functioning within the academic milieu. Most often, if executive functioning is discussed, it is generally in the context of disabilities, that is, executive dysfunction, or what happens when executive functioning goes awry. This is a shocking omission, considering what we know about brain development and the critical role of executive functioning in the brain's ability to learn.

So, how do we develop a brain that is good at learning? And what does it even mean to be good at learning? The notion of learning as an ability or a process that can be refined is a relatively recent concept. It's an understanding that is decades in the making, breaking through the landscape of older, more rigid models that viewed learning not as a process but as a linear scale based on inborn genetic traits. These traditional theories of learning rely on the outdated perception that one's ability to learn and succeed in the classroom and the workplace depends solely on a person's inborn, unchangeable intelligence: their IQ (an abbreviation for the vague term "intelligence quotient").

What Is Your IQ?

In the modern age, the IQ is still a respected metric of gauging an individual's intellectual functioning, but it has been de-mystified due to many decades of controversy and more rigorous scientific inquiry regarding what IQ really represents, what it can actually predict about a person, and whether there are inherent biases (cultural or otherwise) in the way that it is measured.

Many parents and teachers of exceptionally bright children with "high IQs" know that these students can present with all sorts of other behaviors that make learning a challenge for them. For example, these students can present as "unmotivated" or unwilling to put in the effort. Alternatively, they are perhaps "too smart for their own good" and/or averse to challenging themselves, preferring to take shortcuts in their work or find the easy way out. What accounts for the disparity between IQ and academic performance? Brainpower and intelligence matter, of course. But for the learning brain, it is not the only—or even the biggest!—factor at play.

Besides the rise in understanding of the neurobiological workings of the brain that underlie successful learning (i.e., the domains of working memory, self-control, and mental flexibility that compose executive functioning), our focus has shifted toward these other, more elusive qualities in students that account for success. The backlash to IQ has brought heavy hitters to the forefront to replace its use as an influential predictor to achievement and success.

The most convincing and promising of these heavy hitters are theories that consider a student's overall orientation and approach to learning: does the student have the *right* mindset that allows her to integrate, process, and learn from her environment? And is she willing and motivated to persist in the challenge of learning? These factors, crystallized in Carol Dweck's concept of growth mindset and Angela Duckworth's concept of grit, have been identified front and center as influential predictors of learning and academic success. They both argue in diverse ways that, aside from cognitive abilities, there are also "non-cognitive abilities" that supply the gateway for academic success.

Smart, Smarter, Smartest

To understand how revolutionary and powerful these ideas are in terms of disrupting the traditional ways of thinking about intelligence and ability, it is necessary to briefly journey through the story of IQ that has shaped theories of intelligence for nearly a century. Since the first paper-and-pencil test emerged to assess a student's ability, we have been consumed with having a number that determines our intelligence. And we don't want just any number, but a single, whole number that is easy to read and interpret and feeds the human impulse for easy comparison between individuals.

In 1904, French psychologists, Alfred Binet and Theodore Simon, were commissioned to develop a test that could separate those who could succeed in the school system from non-learners. In doing so, Binet and Simon developed the world's first pen- and-paper IQ test. Their thirty-question test of language and abstract concepts, upon which all of today's intelligence tests are built, was intended to assess those who would do well in an academic setting.

Years later, we have been consumed by a number that— allegedly—determines our learning capacity. Numbers are powerful. They present a means of objective ranking (on a numerical scale), which can *then* be turned into labels and categories—and which can then be used to make judgments about a student's (or a whole school's) performance and future. But the issues with IQ as a definitive and comprehensive determinant of intelligence are vast and well documented, rooted largely in pointing out the inherent cultural biases of the test questions and range of acceptable answers. Past predictors of academic success and the traditional research model of academic achievement all lean heavily on intelligence as the key predictor. But the truth is that IQ has been so used and abused that it soured on the very scientists who developed the construct in the first place. Imagine that! Even the original researchers who developed the most widely used intelligence tests believed that IQ was not the only measure that matters.

Within a decade of creating of the first intelligence scale, Binet noted, "A few modern philosophers … assert that an individual's intelligence is a fixed quantity, a quantity that cannot be increased. We must protest and react against this brutal pessimism. ... With practice, training, and above all, method, we can manage to increase our attention, our memory, our judgment and literally to become more intelligent than we were before."

IQ Loses Rank

Executive functioning, grit, and growth mindset: although these terms came into use long after Binet's time, the ideas themselves—that cognitive skills in addition to a temperament willing to improve and persist are truer predictors of success— are actually as old as the notion of IQ itself. And yet, numbers continued to rule. The emphasis on scoring and testing has created a huge amount of friction in educational policy that has yet to find footing in how best to assess the progress of students in a way that doesn't reduce a child's development to easily rankable and categorizable numbers.

One of the world's leading experts on intelligence who created the concept of multiple intelligences, Harvard's Dr. Howard Gardner, became so discouraged by our emphasis on test scores that he wrote in the tenth anniversary edition of his groundbreaking *Frames of Mind*, "First of all try to forget that you have ever heard of the concept of intelligence as a single property of the human mind, or that instrument called the intelligence test, which purports to measure intelligence."

This is not to say that intelligence doesn't matter, simply that it is not the *only* thing that matters. Tests of IQ formulate that number based on a wide range of subtests that tap several cognitive domains, including verbal comprehension, fluid and crystallized intelligence, working memory, processing speed, organization and sequencing, visual-spatial abilities, and many more. The value of these tests is indisputable as a diagnostic tool for psychologists and trained clinicians to better understand the overall functioning of individuals. However, to take a single composite number—IQ—as the be-all-end-all can be reductive and damaging for students, particularly when given a single number without context. It places a ceiling on expectations for a child or prevents access to more enriching and challenging environments that she may, in fact, thrive in.

Ask a Kindergarten Teacher

IQ or "general intelligence" or "brain power" or whatever you want to call it—it matters, certainly. But there needs to be increased attention to what information it can provide about a student, what that number is used for, and what intelligence and/or academic success looks like at different age groups. As young children enter the classroom for the first time, there are more important neurocognitive skills than composite IQ that play a fundamental role in a child's academic achievement. Unsurprisingly, this is something that many educators already know and recognize, although we have yet to fully integrate this knowledge into our educational culture.

In a survey conducted by the National Center for Education Statistics asking kindergarten teachers to name the "essential" and "most important" characteristics for academic readiness, the overwhelming majority of teachers surveyed (upwards of 60 percent and on some items as many as 87 percent) pointed to skills associated with self-regulation, attention, working memory, inhibition, and organization/sequencing, that is, skills associated with executive functioning. These skills included children's abilities to follow directions and not be disruptive of class, communicate their needs, wants, and thoughts verbally, as well as show sensitivity to other children. In contrast, items that might otherwise be construed as traditional markers of intelligence, such as a child's amount of academic knowledge (e.g., the alphabet or basic counting) before entering school were much lower on the list.

Clancy Blair, a developmental psychologist at New York University who has extensively studied the development of executive functions in young children, has written that the school classroom presents a "distinct context within which specific regulatory demands are made of children ... Differences among children in the capacity for regulation within this environment as well as differences in supports for children's self-regulatory attempts both within and without this environment, are important to conceptualizations of readiness that view the transition to school within an ecological framework." Thus, within highly demanding, fast-paced large classroom environments, students must rely on specific neurocognitive skills (working memory, processing and organizing information, mental flexibility, etc.) that enable learning to take place. Furthermore, the amount of *support* and *scaffolding* a child has regarding developing and nurturing these neurocognitive skills plays a critical role in that child's ability to adjust to and be successful in a classroom environment.

Beyond IQ

There has been protracted distancing from intelligence as the core determinant of a child's abilities and academic success, though it has been slow to hit the educational mainstream. Executive functioning is a clear frontrunner, with ever-increasing evidence indicating its fundamental role in the learning process. Yet, barriers have remained in bringing it into practice in the classroom. In tandem with the promising research on executive functioning and academic performance, education has begun to embrace personality and temperament traits, most often described as non-cognitive competencies as important determinants to learning. In fact, hundreds of school organizations have adopted these philosophies and infused them within their existing curricula.

The examination and assessment of non-cognitive abilities has been a long time coming, presciently predicted not only by Alfred Binet, but also Romanian-American psychologist, David Wechsler, the architect of several of the most reputable and most widely used assessments measuring intelligence and academic achievement. Wechsler's assessments have become the gold standard of evaluating children's abilities in the educational world, although it is likely that Wechsler himself did not anticipate how his tests would be overused and, at times, misguided. In fact, in 1950, Wechsler was quoted saying: "First, that factors other than intellectual contribute to achievement in areas where, as in the case of learning, intellectual factors have until recently been considered uniquely determinate and, second, that these other factors have to do with functions and abilities hitherto considered traits of personality. Among those partially identified so far are factors relating primarily to the cognitive functions like drive, persistence, will, and perseveration, or in some instances, the aspect of temperament that pertain to interests and achievement."

Wechsler clearly was ahead of his time in understanding and embracing a holistic approach to learning. Seventy years later, non-cognitive abilities in their impact on learning and development have finally been recognized as central components to academic success. The most popular of these constructs are growth mindset and grit, which have been firmly established as influential predictors of learning and general success. Both concepts will be explored more fully in the next couple of sections.

CHAPTER 10
Growth Mindset and Grit

Growth Mindset

Renowned psychologist Carol Dweck has cultivated research on a transformative construct of how individuals' beliefs shape their life, point of view, and ability to succeed. A person's beliefs, she posits, can fall under one of two different "mindsets." These mindsets, growth and fixed, are the root of long-term success and failure. An individual who has a *fixed mindset* can be understood as someone who believes his or her abilities are unchangeable traits, in other words, carved in stone. A person with a fixed mindset thinks that one's own intelligence cannot increase or decrease. Instead, it is a quantity unchanged from the moment one is born. The outcome of a fixed mindset is a person focused on proving his or her intelligence or selectively refraining from opportunities in which failure may be experienced. They avoid challenges that might not supply an outcome validating their inherent abilities, let alone exposing any weakness. Ultimately, a fixed mindset becomes detrimental in moments of adversity and often leads people to shy away from reaching their potential.

Conversely, an individual with a growth mindset believes that one's intelligence, talent, creativity, and even relational abilities like love and friendship can be developed through effort and deliberate practice. Not only are people with this mindset not discouraged by failure, but they also do not actually see themselves as failing in those situations. They see themselves as learning. Failure becomes an opportunity. Moreover, this mindset leads to the type of thinking that says, "A person's true potential is unknown (and unknowable)," and it is impossible to predict the outcome of years of hard work. A growth mindset allows people to improve themselves by asking for help, trying new things, taking risks, accurately assessing their own intelligence, and most importantly, coping with failures productively.

Prime Time Match: Fixed vs. Growth

In life, fixed mindsets are seen throughout our daily lives. Famed baseball manager Billy Bean ruined his baseball career because of his inability to learn from failure. It was not until he became a manager that he evolved to embrace a growth mindset. A Harvard dropout who attempted many unsuccessful businesses is currently a renowned innovator, philanthropist, and founder of one of the largest computer and software companies today. His name? Bill Gates, whose name is synonymous with Microsoft Corporation. He credits his success to his ability to learn from failure and accept his shortcomings as challenges and the need for change, rather than defeat.

In school, students with a fixed mindset protect their egos by avoiding failure or attributing failure to something separate from their natural ability. For example, they blame teachers, external circumstances, etc. They tend to assume intelligence results in effortless learning and that failing a test or assignment signifies being dumb. Students with fixed mindsets believe that learning and the comprehension of material depend on doing so *effortlessly*. Having to apply more effort or put in more time to understand information discourage these students, who interpret the increased effort as a signal that they have reached the limits of their intelligence. In contrast, putting more effort into a task for students with growth mindsets is hardly a deterrent; in fact, they may show *stronger* understanding because of the increase in difficulty.

This dichotomy in thinking was true for students entering pre-med programs at college. Those students with fixed mindsets who were thrown into classes that were harder than any other they had taken were discouraged because they saw their drop in grades as a sign of a lack of intelligence. In contrast, students with a growth mindset instead saw their apparent lack of higher knowledge indicated by lower grades as an opportunity to learn. Once again, the grades of students with a growth mindset improved far more often than those with a fixed mindset.

Course Corrections

Another important distinction that Dweck draws relates to the way those with different mindsets (dissimilar theories of intelligence) deal with corrections after failure. The growth mindset participants were better able to *learn* from their mistakes. When presented with failure (incorrectly answering a question), they paid closer attention to the corrective feedback and engaged more deeply with it. In contrast, the fixed mindset students didn't put as much effort into fixing their errors and understanding the correct response.

This was further proven on a surprise second test, during which participants were assessed on all the questions they answered incorrectly. Growth mindset students, having used more resources to process the negative feedback, performed significantly better than their fixed mindset counterparts, who mentally blew off the corrections. The fixed mindset participants, upon coming face to face with failure, responded by shutting down—even when immediately given the correct information.

One of the more remarkable findings was that not only did the growth mindset participants perform better, but they were also more likely to correct their errors if they were more confident in their first (wrong) answer, meaning they exerted more effort to learn when they were most wrong.

Now, it's fair to point out that this study was produced within the confines of a lab and asked simple questions that do not quite correspond to the knowledge needed in school, social, and/or professional environments. But the takeaway is that having a fixed mindset offers limited means of overcoming a setback or failure; indeed, *it actively makes it harder to learn from mistakes.* When receiving a graded test, a student with a fixed mindset only sees the grade; a student with a growth mindset sees the grade and then goes to the teacher's corrections to understand and learn from his or her errors.

With her theories firmly backed by decades of research, Dweck implores parents, teachers, and coaches to tell their children to love challenges and meet them head on instead of praising success only. As a result, schools and society at large have embraced the growth mindset construct, and rightly so. Helping students develop the adaptability to weather failure and "pick themselves up from a fall" to continue the achievement race is clearly a message we want to infuse in our learning culture. However, a growth mindset itself is not enough. It is important but not sufficient to develop optimal learners.

Grit Construct (the Next Heavy Hitter)

West Point graduates about 25 percent of the officers in the U.S. Army. The criteria for admission to West Point depends heavily on their Whole Candidate Score, which includes SAT scores, class rank, proven leadership ability, and physical aptitude. Even with such a rigorous and highly selective admissions process, about one in twenty cadets drops out during the summer of training before their first academic year. Duckworth et al. were curious to understand what variables best predicted a new recruit's staying power.

Each cadet was given a very short Grit questionnaire in the first two or three days of summer, along with all the other psychological tests that West Point requires during enrollment. At the end of summer training, as expected, recruits dropped out, and Duckworth checked the data. Ironically, the worst measure to predict dropout was the Whole Candidate Score. There was no predictive relationship between admissions score and whether the cadet would drop out (although it was the best predictor of later grades, military performance, and physical performance). Not surprisingly, grit was the best predictor of which cadets would stick around through that first difficult summer.

In another study among Ivy League students, Duckworth found that students with higher IQs tended to have less grit than their peers who scored lower on an intelligence test. Students who were not as bright as their peers "compensate by working harder and with more determination." And their effort paid off: The grittiest students—not the smartest ones—had the highest GPAs.

So, what is grit exactly?

Angela Duckworth describes grit as a temperament-related trait, saying that it is not about the *ability to act*, but more about the *willingness to commit to action*. Grit is associated with long-term, lifetime educational attainment and professional success; grit predicts the completion of challenging goals despite obstacles and setbacks. Grit predicts success over and beyond talent. When you consider individuals of equal talent, the grittier ones do better. Duckworth adds that having grit includes "sticking with things over the very long term until you master them." She describes the salient advantage to gritty individuals is their stamina—they approach achievement as a marathon.

At the Scripps National Spelling Bee, the grittiest contestants were the most likely to advance to the finals—at least in part because they studied longer, not because they were smarter or were better spellers. Interestingly, practice activities that spellers rated as more pleasurable and less effortful (e.g., reading for pleasure or being quizzed by their parents) were dramatically less predictive of spelling performance. Instead, it was the hardest, least pleasurable practice that really paid off—and the grittiest kids who could do more of it. So, essentially, no pain, no gain. Those overachieving masochists who can endure the worst study torture will win!

CHAPTER 11
All It Takes Is the 2 Gs!

Children who have more of a growth mindset tend to be grittier. The correlation isn't perfect, but it is likely that what makes someone gritty is having a growth mindset. The attitude "I can get better if I try harder" is likely part of the central ingredients to a tenacious, determined, hard-working person. In fact, if you ask a seasoned teacher about grit and failure, you're likely to hear that they have witnessed many students who struggle only to fail. From their failure, they work hard to learn and develop a tremendous amount of grit, ultimately becoming quite successful in school. However, in the same breath, you will hear that they have had just as many bright students who experience academic challenges, only to give up and not develop grit. Building grit and a growth mindset, for that matter, is not as simple as letting a student fail.

While moderate, positive associations between grit and growth mindset suggest that a growth mindset may contribute to the tendency to sustain effort and commitment toward achieving goals, there are some well-founded criticisms of where these constructs stop short. Grit and a growth mindset are belief systems, albeit important ones. They are not a system of neural network connectivity. They do not provide the essential synaptic communication to allow a student to remember and follow multi-step instructions. They do not provide the neurological activation to avoid distractions, control impulses, or adjust when rules change.

The truth is, grit and a growth mindset suppose the mental fortitude and mental flexibility that enable us to recover and grow from failure. Let's be clear. We are talking about failure that occurred despite our efforts. We expect that children (and adults) are actually trying when they failed and feel singed by that failure. Apathy is not part of the fixed or growth mindset equation.

The growth mindset orients a student toward learning, but it doesn't provide the skills to do so. On the one hand, if you have the organizational, regulatory, and information pro-cessing skills but don't orient yourself to implement them optimally, then academic success will be a limited pursuit. On the other hand, even if you are ready and eager to learn and excited by challenges, having a weak working memory, impulse control difficulties, and rigid tendencies will impair your efforts to achieve.

So, we know that having grit and a growth mindset propel a student in the direction of learning, but once that student is there, how do we ensure that learning occurs in the best possible way? Success requires healthy, well-developed executive functioning abilities, alongside a willingness and desire to learn from any potential setbacks. While one can adopt or develop a grit and growth mindset when learning, doing, etc., if the neurobiological foundations to that learning are not firing on all synaptic cylinders, no matter how growth-minded you feel, learning will not be optimal or successful.

Grit and Growth Mindset,
Meet Your Frenemy: Sisyphus

According to the Greek myth, Sisyphus is condemned to roll a rock to the top of a mountain, only for the rock to roll to the bottom every time. Let us momentarily suspend the philosophical and existential musings of the Sisyphean life (Albert Camus for another day) and view this myth a bit more topically. Sisyphus is a gritty, hard-working rock roller. He toils and strains to push the rock up a hill. He reaches temporary success, only for it roll back down: failure, once again. But failure does not deter him! This is a growth mindset. I fail; therefore, I grow! I must keep trying to push that heavy boulder up the hill. To what end? Too much grit? Is more grit always better?

There are contexts in which grit begets lower achievement. For instance, grittier individuals may be less open to information that contradicts their present beliefs, or they may be otherwise handicapped by judgment and decision-making biases. Further, grittier individuals, by staying the course, may sometimes miss new opportunities because they are so focused on their original goal.

Sisyphus, Meet Dashrath the Mountain Man:
When Grit Is Coupled with Executive Functioning

A goal without a plan is just a wish—Antoine de Saint-Exupery.

Working hard for the sake of working hard is Sisyphean futility. A plan must be in place—a plan that is executed with flexibility, self-control, and the forethought to think about the consequences.

In 1960, in Bihar, India, a man named Dashrath Manjhi suffered the loss of his wife after an accident. Her condition was treatable, although treatment was impossible to pursue because the nearest town with a doctor was 44 miles away from their village. The distance could have been far shorter, if not for a mountain between the village and the town. Dashrath did not want anyone else to suffer the same fate as his wife. So he did the unthinkable. He undertook the Herculean task of single-handedly carving a 360-foot-long, 25-foot-high, 30-foot-wide road out of the Gehlour Hills with a hammer, chisel, and nails.

From 1960 to 1982, working day and night for a total of **22 years**, Dashrath toiled with true grit, reducing the distance between Atri and Wazirganj from 44 miles to just 4 miles. Ultimately, with a clear plan and committed approach to solving a life-changing problem, Dashrath was able to channel his profound grit to achieve a monumental accomplishment.

Grit and Growth Mindset vs. Executive Functioning

The research and literature show both a growth mindset and grit to be impressively influential to optimal learning and success. While it is clear that they do pack quite a punch in our ever-evolving quest to maximize our potentials and our children's, they fail to show how those skills can actually develop. There's a bit of a naiveté regarding how we instill these characteristics in our children. Starting with the basics, shouldn't it be obvious that our brains must have the proper neural foundations to develop both grit and a growth mindset? In fact, one can make the argument that you must have the executive functioning skills to develop a growth mindset and grit.

To develop a growth mindset, one must show the mental flexibility to cope and adapt with failure. Growth-minded individuals can take on different perspectives, tolerate being wrong, search for solutions to improve themselves, and be flexible about their abilities. Moreover, a working memory is essential to adapting, as individuals need to be able to recall their experiences on their neural drafting table to apply knowledge and experience to create a new situation and outcome. The encouragement of a growth mindset to view setbacks and failures as opportunities to learn and improve buttresses the motivational and volitional aspects of grit and the ability to find and pursue new goals when others fail. Likewise, to show grit, one undoubtedly must show self-control. One must resist temptation, maintain focus, delay gratification.

Duckworth does acknowledge that grit and self-control are similar concepts. Self-control is the short-term ability to resist temptations and, say, get your schoolwork done; grit is what takes you the distance. It's about "passion and effort sustained over years." She describes self-control as tightly coupled with everyday success, whereas grit is more tightly coupled with exceptional achievements that take decades or a lifetime to accomplish. Clearly, to reach those exceptional achievements, one must demonstrate the self-control required every day (e.g., Dashrath the Mountain Man). Duckworth also makes the distinction that self-control is a skill that can be improved with training and practice, while grit is much more about volitional motivation. Again, while Duckworth skirts the issue a bit, it is clear that one cannot engage in long-term (grit) goals without the benefit of self-control to facilitate the process.

Likewise, Dweck also recognizes that cognitive skills are just as important and proceeds to incorporate the term "academic tenacity" to address the limitations of a growth mindset. Dweck continues to say that academic tenacity is comprised of a student's mindset as well as the skills that allow students to set short-term concerns aside to withstand challenges and setbacks en route to longer-term or higher-order goals. The skills she is referring to include strategies, such as planning, monitoring, and modifying actions. If I am not mistaken, that sounds a lot like executive functioning. These skills must exist for the value of growth-minded thinking to be effective. Ultimately, Dweck acknowledges that having a growth mindset is one aspect of a complicated learning process. More importantly, she recognizes that key skills (better known as "executive functioning") are valuable to the process.

It is clear that having a growth mindset and grit are invaluable characteristics for one's potential success. And while they are undoubtedly integral to learning, they do not supersede the value of executive functioning and its implications for learning. Academic success cannot occur without executive functioning skills. You can work hard and emotionally embrace a new challenge, but if you cannot cognitively encode, organize, and self-regulate your learning experience, you will not be able to consistently progress within an academic environment.

And yes, some will argue the comparison or hierarchical understanding of executive functioning, a growth mindset, and grit is a bit of the chicken or the egg. It may be true that the grittier you are, the more likely you will activate and reactivate the neurons to cement the neural architecture of executive functioning. That said, executive functioning skills have been shown to appear as early as six months of age. It is hardly imaginable that both grit and a growth mindset appear so early (but maybe they do?).

Whether growth mindset or grit arrive before executive functioning, when it comes to the very essence of learning, the neural pathways in working memory, self-control, and cognitive flexibility require varying degrees of activation to process information. Executive functioning may be more important at the start, but a growth mindset and grit are obviously needed to scaffold the learning process. In fact, a growth mindset and grit are most valuable in helping students tolerate discomfort when learning something new. A growth mindset and grit help children to embrace multiple stages in the learning process and value the journey of learning. Executive functioning gives children the ability to engage in that process day in and day out.

CHAPTER 12

Action Potential

It is firmly established that IQ no longer sits on the throne of learning. Again, while it does have a place in the royal family of education, it is not king. Rodolfo Mendoza-Denton, associate professor of psychology at University of California, Berkeley, aptly stated, "People have aptitudes that are undeniable. ... We can't all be geniuses, but we can all access learning."

Whatever terminology, constructs, scientific terms, and trendy language are used, it is obvious that optimal learning needs both psychological and neurological competencies. Grit, a growth mindset, and executive functioning are at the helm. They define our **action potential**. They define a child's learning ability, performance, engagement, and motivation to learn. If we could maximize the development of all three, perhaps we could optimize a level of learning (and confidence in learning) never thought possible. More boldly, optimizing all three variables likely provides the most powerful insights to assess how well a child can learn and succeed.

The Formula: Executive Functioning + Grit + Growth Mindset = Action Potential

Action potential is the essence of learning through an active and interactive process of executive functioning, grit, and a growth mindset. It serves as the evolving blueprint that begins with our DNA and is shaped through our environmental experiences. Ultimately, understanding a child's action potential will provide essential information about their readiness, receptivity, and long-term accessibility toward learning. Simply put, a child's action potential is at the heart of how ready, how well, and how much he or she will learn. With the above in mind, the next sections will be specific to understanding critical developmental and academic stages of executive functioning. In addition, important milestones related to growth mindset and grit will be explored.

Executive Functioning and Infancy

During infancy to late toddlerhood, the brain is developing and pruning neural connections to manage the onslaught of new information. These young brains are learning to hold information in mind, contain their impulses, and think flexibly for the first time in their young neural lives. While all three components of one's action potential are important in all phases and stages of school, certain skills will be more important during specific critical periods.

While discrete structures in executive functioning are not seen until later infancy, the foundation to this development begins in the first hours, days, and weeks of life. Specifically, early parent/child bonding provides the security that babies need to help them cope with their new world. Research has shown that babies who experience regular skin-to-skin contact with their parents coped with stress better, slept better, and showed stronger growth in their brains, including maturation of the prefrontal cortex (i.e., the frontal lobes!).

Clearly, the process to develop healthy executive functioning begins from birth via attachment and extends into a secure interactive environment of nurturing and enrichment. Moreover, understanding the various stages of development and when enrichment is optimal provides a general framework for developing the building blocks to learning. Let's begin with working memory.

Working Memory

Working memory appears at around seven to eight months of age, although the neural process begins to take form as early as four months. Consider the classic, popular baby game of peekaboo. Peekaboo is so simple, yet complex. It illustrates the development of object permanence, in which babies begin to realize that an object still exists, even if covered up. In other words, Daddy's face disappears and reappears like magic. However, as infants develop, they realize that Daddy's face never disappears but exists behind his hands. This cognitive milestone underlies the development of working memory. Infants begin to have the ability to hold symbolic representations in their minds that help them orchestrate their intended actions. Playing games such as peekaboo and jack in the box prime an infant's brain to develop and fortify the essential neural network of working memory.

During the latter half of infancy, babies not only develop the ability to remember that obscured objects (e.g., a toy hidden under a cloth) are still there, but they also develop the ability to *utilize* that information and coordinate their actions in a sequence toward some intended end (e.g., remove the cloth and grasp the toy). Functionally, this means that babies can use their burgeoning mental drafting tables to execute simple means-to-ends tasks and implement two-step plans. For example, if their favorite toy is hidden under their blankie, babies can retain this information while executing a plan to remove their blankie to successfully grasp their toy. Likewise, when playing jack in the box or similar pop-up toys, babies begin to execute actions such as remembering that pulling the green lever will make the lion pop up and pushing the red circle will make the panda pop up.

At around one year, babies show a marked increase in their ability to hold information for longer periods of time before the information is lost. This capacity continues to improve, with major gains and advances occurring in late nursery and pre-school years.

Self-Control

As early as six months, babies can show very rudimentary response inhibition, albeit inconsistently. Response inhibition means stopping oneself from performing an action that would be inappropriate for a given situation. For example, when commanded (or reprimanded) not to touch the electric socket, babies can suppress the temptation to reach out and touch it— at least for a time.

In later infancy, other aspects of self-control begin to emerge, including sustained, goal-directed focus: that is, maintaining attention on a task or to a command despite brief delays and distractions. Revisiting the jack-in-the-box toy serves as a good example. In addition to helping working memory develop, the simplicity of jack in the box requires that the baby wait for the intended surprise. Providing opportunities for the baby to regulate his or her focus and tolerate tension in anticipation of a surprise is a great builder of self-control.

Mental Flexibility

While working memory and self-control are closely connected (albeit distinct) in infancy and early childhood, the development of mental flexibility emerges closer to the preschool years. It is a relative latecomer on the scene. Prior to that, the very first "soft" signs of emerging mental flexibility occur in late infancy in babies' ability to engage in joint attention. This refers to a baby's ability to look in the same direction of someone else's gaze.

In other words, if you are holding your nine-month-old baby and change the direction of your gaze to stare at a person walking through the door, you baby will turn her head in the direction you are staring. Between twelve and eighteen months, your baby will look in the direction you are pointing (instead of your finger). She will also point with her finger to draw your attention to something of interest. Most strikingly, research shows that toddlers at twenty months of age who showed the highest rates of joint attention scored the highest on the theory of mind at three and half years of age. As previously shown, the theory of mind is the ability to see others' point of view, understand alternative perspectives, and engage in flexible thinking.

Grit and Growth Mindset

Have you ever met an unmotivated infant? Infants by the nature of survival are curious creatures who seek stimulation. Yes, some cry more than others, and some get frustrated more easily than others, but we, as parents, have a significant role in creating a culture of grit and growth mindsets. We know that the foundation of grit requires the cognitive ability to show self-control as well as the mental fortitude to understand the importance of persevering.

While infants clearly do not have the self-awareness to understand perseverance, we can certainly create an environment to nurture the beginning stages of self-control and, more importantly, the frustration tolerance that underlies the development of self-control. In fact, when parents ask how early self-control can be encouraged, I typically respond, "At birth!" Of course, I say this facetiously, but my intention is to prime parents to understand that self-control starts with the ability to both recognize and gain comfort with providing opportunities of optimal frustration.

Sigmund Freud and Heinz Kohut developed the theory of optimal frustration in early development. They posited that children experience frustration from birth, beginning with the caregiver-child interaction. As any parent can attest, typical parenting experiences involve some mix of falling short of a child's demands and overindulging them. Freud and Kohut defined "optimal frustration" as falling somewhere between the two extremes of overindulgence and deprivation. In other words, a child develops healthily through a series of adequately challenging experiences. Freud described it best by stating that it is a frustration that is neither so intense as to be traumatic nor so minimal as to be insignificant.

The experience of tolerable disappointment leads to the establishment of internal structures that supply the basis for self-soothing, that is, the preliminary structures of self-control. While any parent can attest to the fact that experiencing the duress of their infant, toddler, or child of any age can be agonizing, it is important to understand how optimal frustration even in infancy can give a child the opportunity to develop lifelong skills. This may be easier said than done, but may make parents think twice when they are rushing to their child's aid for every whimper and cry. Likewise, there's something to be said for parents who want to toughen their kids up. We are talking about optimal frustration, not deprivation.

As with grit, a growth mindset during the early infant/toddler years benefits from the emergence of mental flexibility as well as general enrichment provided within a child's environment. Specifically, understanding and building upon optimal frustration as well as helping children develop independent problem-solving skills help these psychological structures emerge. In infancy, however, babies will not understand the concepts of self and other. (Recall, children don't begin to develop their theory of mind until around age three.) Accordingly, it is important to be mindful of mental flexibility as a latecomer compared to working memory and self-control. This does not mean a growth mindset should be shelved for later use; however, it requires that parents be more aware of an infant's and young toddler's cognitive and developmental limitations. At this stage, providing opportunities to develop and enrich their joint attention skills could prove useful in fortifying mental flexibility, the foundation for a growth mindset.

Executive Functioning in Toddlerhood
and the Emergent Preschooler

Moving past the delicate infancy stage, toddlerhood is a critical period. With language steadily emerging and an awareness of the world that surrounds them, toddlers are at the epicenter of one of the most important stages of human development. This is by far the toughest age for most parents because of the wild variability in development; no two toddlers are alike. Yet, this is also one of the more important times in their neural development. Remember that, during toddlerhood, children are continuing to fortify their working memory capacities as well as beginning to develop (and conveniently regress regarding) their self-control skills. They are also developing and showcasing their lack of cognitive flexibility.

We know that imaginary play, storytelling, matching/sorting, and many traditional toddlerhood and common preschool activities are invaluable during this period. More important and typically less emphasized are the metacognitive activities crucial to maximizing a child's executive functioning during these common preschool activities. For example, a newly emerging program, Tools of the Mind, follows the brain-based learning model of reinforcing cognitive skills that are on the edge of emerging, particularly those of executive functioning in young, developing brains.

One of Tools of the Mind's central foci is the use of play planning as an instructional strategy to develop self-regulated learning. A child is asked to provide a brief play plan that describes the role and actions in which he or she will engage during the first few minutes of play. This play plan may describe the intentions of make-believe play or the process by which he or she will undertake an art project. In this process,

working memory and self-regulation skills are being cultivated. Likewise, flexibility is required when the play plans must
be adjusted.

While programs such as Tools of the Mind show promise
in their philosophy and structure, all is not lost if a child's
program does not adhere to such a model. Understanding the
developmental trajectory at this age can allow for maximizing
executive functioning skills when opportunities arise.

Working Memory

During the late toddler to early preschool years, a child's
working memory begins to grow at a rapid pace, like all
neurological functions. The surface area of a child's mental
drafting table expands and permits more complex play,
interactions, and independent behavior. In addition, the
explosion of language and ability for children to verbalize
interests, ideas, and needs (ad nauseam) provide tangible
access to their experience with the world. Working memory
becomes an active system as children learn to classify, sort,
and compare objects in the world by their various characteristics (shape, size, color, use, etc.).

Children at this age also develop an improved ability to
use these pieces of information to achieve a functional and
more specific goal. For example, a child can typically hold two
rules in mind and smoothly demonstrate them (e.g., "place the
red blocks here, and the blue blocks there"). Most notably, one
of the more defining characteristics of children this age—their
propensity to ask caregivers "But why?"—stems in part from
the development of working memory.

Preschool-age children can typically hold in mind information about two temporally separated events, inferring

connections about the events or theorizing aloud about them ("But why?"). The "why" also begins to set the building blocks of mental flexibility in motion. Working memory and cognitive flexibility allow moments of assimilation and accommodation, as described by Piaget.

Because of their increased abilities, the activities and tools to develop and enrich a child's working memory are endless. Games such as "Memory," in which children take turns flipping an array of cards to find a pair are classic builders of working memory skills. However, games offer just one dimension. Social play also maintains a strong footing in working memory skills (among other cognitive faculties). Symbolic (pretend) play is a champion of integrating multiple cognitive skills requiring complex thinking to create a successful experience. The creation of characters, roles, and rules all require working memory to keep track of this imaginary landscape. Likewise, reading and storytelling allow children to maintain and manipulate information in their working memories. Thus, it is a combination of games symbolic play, and related interactions that are important facilitators to stretch a child's working memory.

Self-Control

Around three and four years of age, children show other increases in self-control as their capacity to control their behavior on command emerges: for example, being able to delay eating a treat—cue the marshmallow experiment!—or use their inside voice when excited. In fact, children at this age show exponential growth in their ability to resist distractions, which peaks around their fourth birthday. From then on, the rate of development in self-control slows and becomes more stepwise until age seven. It is not a coincidence that the marshmallow experiment and the Dunedin study in New Zealand also evaluated self-control and other cognitive skills in this age group.

This is not to say that children are self-regulated machines. Anyone who lives with children between the ages of three and five know that self-control is really an exhaustive dance between regression and progression. It is by far the one emerging executive function skill that creates a tear-your-hair-out factor with parents because of the variability displayed. "Tommy, don't hit your brother," and "Claire, stop playing with the toilet water!" are relatable examples that showcase the self-control language we impose on children at this age and the persistent inconsistency of the development of self-control.

In fact, this age group presents more behavioral management interventions than any other. In other words, sticker charts, bribery, and incentives become the currency for developing self-regulation skills. However, behavioral plans are limited in scope, as they are typically imposed to extinguish behaviors because of a lack of self-control. It is also important to consider and partake in activities that foster self-control skills and create a positive experience with play and engagement.

Movement games are classic developers of self-control at this age. Freeze games, duck-duck-goose, red-light-green light, and *Simon Says* exercise children's self-control skills. Likewise, quieter activities such as yoga, playing "statue," waiting one's turn to use a toy, and standing in line at the grocery store enlist self-control. Moreover, as previously described, providing opportunities for children to create play plans to organize the intentions of their actions can serve as excellent activators of self-regulation skills.

Mental Flexibility

By preschool, the early developmental stages of the theory of mind (the understanding that other people have different perspectives, beliefs, feelings, and knowledge) begin to reliably emerge. Children at this age are still, as Piaget described, egocentric and tend to experience their environments only in terms of their own point of view. However, their ability to comprehend others' perspectives and emotional states comes more easily, when encouraged by an adult or when it is advantageous. While there are different mechanisms and terminology that describe this process, Piaget best illustrates the emergence of mental flexibility through the aforementioned process of assimilation and accommodation.

With the rapid emergence of language and working memory, children are in a constant state of reorganizing their understanding of their world. Their persistent question of "Why" becomes central to this process, in which children are reframing and resolving discrepancies between what they already know and what they discover. Attempts to resolve these discrepancies force a child to change viewpoints and allow alternative solutions. In other words, deactivating prior perspectives and expanding them to include and accommodate a new piece of information are the core process of mental flexibility.

We do not need to look too much further than the rules of language to understand how flexible thinking intersects with important developmental skills. In fact, mental flexibility is a requirement for children to learn the rules of language. For example, as children learn verb tenses, they begin to internalize rules, such as the way to put most words in the past tense is to add "-ed" to the end. Children must also understand there are exceptions to those rules. The past tense of "go" is "went"; kids start with "go-ed," before switching to "went." Engaging in flexible thinking lets children integrate this rule within their repertoire. Flexible thinkers can easily use both the rules and exceptions of language. With that in mind, one can easily see how flexible thinking also plays a role in learning foreign languages. In fact, acquiring a foreign language at an early age helps foster the development of mental flexibility.

Beyond the verbal categorizations and symbolic understanding of the world, functional behavior also relies on the emergence and improvement of mental flexibility. Parents endure various moments of mental strain in child rearing, and while we can all argue the finer points of our sanity being tested, no one will argue that the experience of task transitions with small children is a form of torture. For example, getting small children from dinner to a bath, then out of a bath, into their pajamas, and into bed is a Sisyphean sport. Each task requires the ability for children to transition from one activity to the next, shift gears, and change their engagement (and compliance). While that may sound easy (and expected), the neurological mechanisms that are needed for transitions to occur smoothly are rooted in mental flexibility.

Adjusting and conforming to environmental demands forces children to engage in transitions of their behavior and expectations. These same neurological mechanisms are practiced in game playing, turn taking, and sharing. Think of the famous game of Candyland. Children move their players through the maze of colors dictated by cards they pick up each turn. At any moment, their card could dictate that they return to an earlier point. Chutes and Ladders also follows a similar model. This may frustrate most, but it does require that children learn to be flexible in their ability to adjust to changes in their experiences. In the early days and years of preschool, mental flexibility is and should be a constant state of practice. Helping children improve their ability to make transitions through changes in their activities, understanding the viewpoints of their peers and teachers, as well as managing and tolerating unexpected changes have significant impact on mental flexibility. Moreover, these experiences can be fostered in a variety of settings. Gym time, music, and art enhance the emergence of mental flexibility, which is why it is tied so closely to creativity.

Grit and Growth Mindset

Our cognitive flexibility develops and improves when we are consistently exposed to multiple viewpoints and perspectives. It also increases when we can assimilate multiple layers of knowledge that interconnect facts, rules, skills, procedures, plans, and deep conceptual principles. As children begin to become aware of the self and other, narrations of perspective taking become valuable. As previously described, Piaget observed the process as assimilation and accommodation in which children begin to develop these abilities. In addition, as language is emerging and children are exploring the world with greater awareness, we have a prime opportunity to instill perseverance and effort into their actions. Helping children to recognize when failure occurs eases their development, especially when they can understand that there are multiple ways of accomplishing a goal or action.

Moreover, helping children develop and understand alternative viewpoints and recognizing and creating solutions for daily dilemmas all become important teaching moments. For example, when a child is trying to make a structure with blocks that repeatedly falls over, simple narrations can change a child's experience of their failure. "I see that you're getting frustrated with your blocks, but I like how you're not giving up! Let's think about building a different way—maybe try the smaller blocks." Praise children's effort instead of the outcome. Of course, young children might reach peak frustration and need to step away from a task, which is perfectly acceptable and just as effective a strategy in helping develop their persistence. Stepping away allows a child to emotionally regroup and reassess how to improve his or her approach.

Ultimately, parents' language matters. Avoid fixed mindset language: that was so easy, you must be so smart, you're so good at Legos, etc. Instead, praise the effort and process, including what it took to develop those skills. So, are we praising mediocrity in this instance? Many (type A) parents will scoff when discussing the "acceptance" of failure with their children. It is important to keep in mind that a growth mindset does not celebrate failure, but celebrates how to rebound and learn from it.

In addition to task persistence, social/emotional experiences can also foster foundations of grit and a growth mindset. During opportune moments, pointing out when another child is crying and talking about the feelings he or she may be experiencing can foster perspective taking. This can be especially important if your child was the one who accidentally caused the other child to become upset. Help your child problem solve situations to make someone feel better. If another child is upset, ask your child what he or she could do to help that friend. Give her some ideas, like going to get an ice pack, helping the other child off the ground, or finding something fun for the child to do.

Reading age-appropriate books and discussing how the characters may be feeling is another way to facilitate these skills. Identify the characters' emotions and talk about why the characters feel that way and how you know they are experiencing those feelings (e.g., he is smiling; he found his toy, etc.). More importantly, discuss your own emotions. Label your own feelings throughout the day and talk about why you're experiencing the feelings described. If you have negative emotions, talk about what would make you feel better. You will be surprised at how those discussions will also change your viewpoints and interactions.

A New Stage: Transitioning into the Classroom

The early years of life, from birth to around age five, set the stage for what will be the most challenging transition of a young child's life: entering the formal schooling environment. For children who did not attend daycare or preschool, this is the first time they are in an environment surrounded by their peers, without their parents, and are to engage in specific, guided tasks for extended periods of time every day. In traditional programs, this also means adjusting to a format of structured periods focusing on learning and listening, exploring, interrogating, and navigating early emotional and social quandaries. The demands of this environment are immense and unprecedented in childhood; thus, the ability of a child to meet expectations depends almost entirely on the cognitive and psychological toolkit that has been built to this point.

At this stage, executive functioning is of the utmost importance. Developmental and school psychologists know this, and teachers know it, too. When asked the most important skills that children require to be successful in the classroom, the majority of kindergarten teachers surveyed by the National Center of Education Statistics *specifically* identified skills related to executive functioning as having greater import than traditional measures, such as phonological skills, vocabulary, and early number sense. These traditional metrics largely reflect "crystallized" knowledge, information that a child has already learned, become familiar and facile with, and can deploy reliably and appropriately.

It is, of course, helpful and necessary to assess what a child knows for the purposes of establishing a baseline in the classroom and identifying a child's foundation level in these academic areas. However, while the early acquisition of these facts often begets the quicker learning of subsequent skills within those domains (e.g., early phonological skills and reading development), the relationship is not one to one. Moreover, having specific types of knowledge going into the classroom does not necessarily say anything about a child's ability to behave and flourish under the specific emotional, regulatory, and attentional demands of the classroom environment.

Of course, while the start of formal schooling is a critical period, this is not to suggest that development after this point stagnates and that the skills children go into the classroom with are what they will have for the rest of their lives: far from it! Strong executive functioning skills will help children to succeed in the classroom, but these brains are still growing and being shaped. The important point here is to eliminate false assumptions that weaknesses in self-control, working memory, perspective taking, and problem solving mean a child is simply not going to be a good learner. Rather, this transition into formal schooling presents a critical period of cognitive growth, and parents and teachers should recognize and emphasize opportunities to foster these underlying foundations of learning.

Grit and a growth mindset also begin to enter the picture in a more dominant manner, particularly as they relate to organically developing the motivation, drive, and interest in learning we hope becomes a lifelong internalized process. From the simplest to most complex activities, engaging and maximizing the development of a toddler/young child's working memory, self-regulation, and cognitive flexibility provides invaluable skills and readies them for more than a decade of learning. Our children will spend the next twelve years (and often longer) in a school environment where their executive functioning skills will be heavily taxed every day. Given what we know about the brain, shouldn't we give them every chance to optimize their experience?

Working Memory

As stated throughout, of all the components of executive functioning, working memory is arguably the most central to initial learning. In fact, research findings indicate that children's working memory skills at five years of age were the best predictor of literacy and numeracy six years later. The ability to engage in learning depends on children's abilities to hold and manipulate information, a skill required for even the simplest of academic tasks (e.g., counting, basic addition, reciting the alphabet, sounding out words, etc.).

In this way, working memory can become a bottleneck in learning over the short and longer term, as children with weaker working memory abilities are slower to pick up information and struggle to retain material from one day to the next. In addition, engaging in simple day-to-day classroom activities such as remembering instructions can become a burdensome challenge that affects participation and active learning. Students may become lost or confused, needing continual guidance from instructors to stay on task and follow directions appropriately.

It is important to highlight that underdeveloped working memory at this stage looks very similar to poor attention, particularly as attention and memory are very closely related. To sustain focus on a task, you must be able to remember what to do and monitor yourself to assess how far you've gotten. Returning briefly to the question of crystallized knowledge versus executive functioning skills, this is where strong working memory skills are undoubtedly a winning ticket.

Studies have demonstrated that, against a wide variety of measures—IQ, early literacy, vocabulary, familial attitudes toward education, etc.—working memory most reliably and consistently predicts academic achievement. Why? Because working memory is foundational to the *capacity* to learn (i.e., to take in, store, and retrieve salient information). When presented with academic material, a child who may not have had as much exposure to it can quickly catch up to and surpass peers who, despite having memorized academic facts early on, may not be able to manipulate and build on that knowledge with the same level of ease. In a way, working memory can be considered a measure of mental *agility*. At a time when foundational skills in reading, writing, and math are forming, it is crucial that these young brains are best equipped to take in, hold, and process the masses of information coming at them.

Self-Control

Enrollment within formal education requires achieving important advances in self-control, namely, in children's capacity to resist distractions, control their behavior and emotions, make decisions about whether their actions are appropriate for a situation, and maintain their focus on a goal or for the duration of a lesson. The very nature of the demands inherent in a structured classroom *reinforces* the development of the aforementioned skills. For example, requiring children to follow basic classroom rules such as raising their hand and waiting their turn to speak, keeping their hands to themselves, walking quietly in the halls, putting away materials once the lesson is over, and playing by the rules in gym class encourages independent skills in self-monitoring, organization, and filtering distractions.

Children at this stage can typically follow simple rules and perform tasks without needing parent or adult supervision—for a time. However, self-monitoring (i.e., the ability to assess one's own behavior and progress toward achieving some goal) and self-awareness have not yet consistently formed, which can derail classroom behavior and, in turn, learning. This process is tightly coupled with working memory skills, as a child's ability to remain on task and work toward a goal depends on his or her abilities to *remember* the steps necessary to achieve it.

As with the growing toddler whose self-regulatory abilities are marked most consistently by inconsistency, providing uniform and structured expectations can strengthen his or her growth in this area. Returning to the idea of behavioral management, many of the same strategies and interventions used by parents at home can be adapted to a group environment to facilitate self-regulation in the classroom. In fact, they largely form the basis of most classroom management strategies. This includes the use of simple, clear, and specific rules that are referenced daily and applicable to all students, thus reinforcing self-monitoring skills. For example, teachers will often repeat behavioral phrases like "Wait your turn to speak," "No talking in the hallway," "Always follow directions," etc. Rules such as these can and should (where appropriate) be made with the guided input of the students themselves to engage in explicit behavioral planning, thus modeling internal planning strategies (i.e., "How should I behave to be successful?"). Teachers can also create activities that foster these skills through partnered projects, learning games, and class lessons.

Mental Flexibility

When structured learning occurs in a group setting, children must process and engage not just with the material in front of them, but also the social environment around them. In toddlerhood and the early preschool years, children are beginning to contend with the understanding that those around them perceive and experience the world differently. By age five, when "formal" learning generally begins, that process is reaching completion.

In one of the most well-known and standard tests of the theory of mind and perspective taking, a child is shown a pencil box and, when prompted, will typically guess that there are pencils inside of it. However, upon opening the box, it is revealed that the box *does not* hold pencils, but some other object—let's say, blocks. Next, the child is asked what a friend who walks into the room and sees the (closed) pencil box might think was inside. The child's answer demonstrates a significant step in his or her social understanding. Younger children, who have not yet developed the understanding that others are not privy to the same information, will typically answer, "Blocks." Conversely, older children who have developed a more complex understanding of perspectives quickly grasp and can deploy an understanding of *differential knowledge*, that someone who hasn't seen inside would have no reason to know that the box is not what it appears to be.

So, what does this mean for the classroom? Social and emotional learning is a parallel, critical process occurring in tandem with traditional learning. At this stage, self-control forms a steady buttress as mental flexibility begins to blossom outright. Thus, the rule setting and creation of classroom-wide expectations discussed previously also create an important space for social understanding to grow and for its cognitive substrates to develop. Consider the widespread use of classroom rules that focus on interpersonal behaviors—"Respect others' personal space and belongings," "Be kind to others," "Treat others the way you would like to be treated," etc. These rules implicitly bolster students' abilities to consider multiple perspectives and how their behaviors and desires may conflict with others.

The social/emotional learning and development taking place at this stage is made possible by improvements in both aspects of mental flexibility—flexible thinking and set shifting. This latter skill is rigorously tested in the formal classroom environment, which requires children to smoothly adapt in a space of continual transitions—between tasks and activities, moving around the classroom (e.g., between floor/rug and tables), between classrooms, as well as the transitions between settings with vastly different expectations and rules (from home to school and back again). The development of these skills particularly varies among children, with some having more difficulty than others in managing the changing demands of their environment, resulting in rigidity, frustration, and stress.

To support young students' abilities to mentally adapt and transition between activities and spaces, teachers should

Social and emotional learning, continued... Increased focus has been placed on the use of formal, evidence-based programs that are centered on social and emotional learning. A leading organization in the field, the Collaborative for Academic, Social, and Emotional Learning (CASEL) has developed program guides for teachers and schools to introduce classroom goals of social and emotional learning. CASEL argues that it is essential to encourage students and young people to not only be good learners and classroom citizens, but also "knowledgeable, caring, responsible, and healthy." And this is backed by experimental research; in one study of 753 children, performance on a standardized test of social competence in kindergarten predicted outcomes 19 years later in education and employment, criminal activity and substance use, as well as mental health. Fostering early abilities in social functioning (which is itself a product of mental flexibility) lays a foundation for lifelong success.

provide as much explicit structuring as possible to "ground" students. For example, allotting a set time for transitions between activities and announcing in advance when these transitions will be taking place ("In five minutes, we're going to wrap up and put the materials away") provides an appropriate framework to fortify flexible thinking with predictable and regular procedures.

Other activities that can support set shifting in the classroom and at home include age-appropriate board and card games that draw upon planning and strategizing. Likewise, the introduction of simple logic/reasoning puzzles and mazes, which require the activation of strategies (and the deactivation of unsuccessful strategies) to succeed, are excellent activities for flexible thinking. The popular board game Checkers requires players to continually assess and adapt their moves as well as anticipate and foresee their opponent's options to win. Likewise, the card game Uno requires players to modify their approach based on which rule is most beneficial for the cards in their hand (either sorting by color or number) as well as utilize other cards to reverse or skip players to better their chances of winning, all the while remembering to be the first to call "Uno!" when any player has one card remaining. While these may seem superficial and/or perfunctory, they create opportunities to instill flexibility in a fun, non-threatening manner.

Grit and Growth Mindset

Although the three core aspects of executive functioning form the foundations that make successful entry into the classroom environment possible, this stage of (literal and figurative) transitions presents new and more frequent situations for both progress and failure. Managing expectations around failure and emphasizing the importance of persistence remain key components of setting early foundations for the development of gritty students. Various, and likely endless, activities exist to foster grit. Creating a classroom (and home) culture that emphasizes the value of grit is critical to influencing this mindset. Even social activities in which children are cheered on to persist with a difficult task can be transformative to give both emotional and cognitive reinforcement.

Like grit, a growth mindset becomes (or should become) an emerging focal point to a child's development during this time. As previously shown, Dweck theorizes that a person's growth mindset is closely related to his or her "theory of intelligence." This is not to be confused with the theory of mind, which refers to individuals' understanding of others' mental abilities and perspectives. Rather, one's theory of intelligence is focused on the self: what individuals believe about their own mental capacities and perspectives *in comparison* to others. The social experience of formal learning and becoming aware of one's performance in relation to peers presents a critical period in shaping early theories about intelligence (and talents). The foundation of a growth mindset is the belief that intelligence is not a fixed trait. Rather, knowledge can be developed and fostered with active effort, and abilities can vary across domains.

A growth mindset and grit seem very commonsensical in their importance for early learners, although educators are not always mindful about who requires more reinforced exposure to this framework of thinking. For bright and quick-learning students who enter the classroom well ahead of their peers regarding crystallized knowledge and the early capacity to process and retain information, early learning often feels easy and effortless. Although this can put children at some advantage in terms of quickly assimilating new information to build on those skills, it is important to recognize the potential for pitfalls of effortless learning.

I cannot help but interject my own professional experiences with this student profile. I have met dozens beyond dozens of students who display an impressive, almost gifted level of intelligence that allowed for an effortless school experience in their early education. These students rarely struggled with concepts, learned foundation skills quickly with minimal to no practice, and seemed to experience success easily. Teachers and parents alike praise the success of these students, only to become surprised and confused when these students take a nosedive as soon as demands increase (often in later grades).

Like the experience of many prodigies, early, effortless success can be a detriment, as it often bypasses the important experiences of developing persistence as well as tolerating and learning from failure. When early, tolerable pitfalls occur, this gives the opportunity for a student to experience discomfort and make natural (non-threatening) adjustments to succeed.

Executive Functioning in Elementary School

Within an educational system that emphasizes problem solving and meaningful instruction, there is a significant increase in the number of tasks that require students to plan, initiate, organize, prioritize, shift, and check their work. In this way, the curricula of formal schooling assume that students are coming to the table equipped with the proper executive functioning skills to manage the imposed demands. Students are expected to come to class prepared with completed homework, engage in active learning, study efficiently, and perform well on tests.

At a developmental level, the relationship between cognitive skills, intrapersonal competencies, and academic performance begins to take shape. Thus, a child's *action potential* at this stage weighs heavily on his or her core executive functioning skills. However, a growth mindset and grit are both now edging closer to equal importance.

While executive functioning sets the stage for learning and forms the means by which children are prepared to manage classroom demands successfully, grit and a growth mindset provide a path toward academic achievement. We are no longer just asking the binary question "Does this child have the neurocognitive skills in place for learning?" We are also asking, "How well is this child learning?" and "How willing is this student to demonstrate what he or she has learned?" While school readiness focuses on priming a child to develop the foundation skills to learn, academic achievement is understanding how a student uses those foundation skills in the learning process.

The relationship between grit and growth mindset becomes increasingly important, especially because of the way both constructs are enmeshed in how *well* students learn. As previously indicated, moderate, positive associations have been found between grit and a growth mindset. In other words, a growth mindset likely contributes in some capacity to the tendency to sustain effort toward and a commitment to goals. Viewing setbacks and failures as opportunities to learn and improve serves to buttress the motivational/volitional aspects of grit and the ability to identify and pursue new goals when others fail.

Working Memory

Children in elementary school exhibit further growth in their abilities to retain and manipulate information. There is an increase in the amount of information able to be stored and the duration for which it can be held. Students can successfully participate in more complex activities and more easily follow multiple-step directives. Related to these developments in working memory are underlying and parallel developments in sustained attention in which students can remain focused longer and process information more efficiently. In addition, middle-school children can now show the reliable employment of memory strategies, for example, repeating information in a list or sequences of numbers aloud.

Consider the development of reading skills, which is clearly a complex neurocognitive process. Working memory plays a crucial, if not the most important, role in this process. For example, auditory working memory allows a student to retrieve and hold on to the sounds that letters make, which in turn helps him or her to sound out new words. In addition, visual working memory gives students the ability to remember what those letter patterns and words look like, so they can recognize them through the decoding process. When properly employed, students begin to read with greater prosody and fluency, as they no longer need to rely on sounding out each word they see.

Similarly, when performing math calculations, students must be able to keep and manipulate numbers in their minds based on the required operative rule. From there, students develop the skills to store information about a word problem in their minds to write a related math problem and execute calculations accordingly. This enables kids to remember mathematical formulas.

The school experience itself places heavy demands on working memory; however, this does not prevent teachers from focusing on maximizing its development. Fostering and fortifying working memory for each classroom experience is vital to ensuring students' ongoing development. Teachers can do this with concrete working memory activities as well as by adjusting their teaching to ensure the activation of working memory skills—for example, reading instructions aloud and having students repeat them or providing a short re-view/preview before teaching a new lesson. Likewise, having students read a passage together and summarize their readings or having students recap their weekends in a journal can foster these skills. Presenting math problems verbally engages students to mentally manipulate numbers and retain these numbers in their minds while fortifying their arithmetic skills.

At home, working memory can be activated by the simple task of discussing the events of a school day. The parental cliché of "How was school today, Sofia?" is almost guaranteed to be followed with the reply "Good" or "OK." However, if parents begin to ask targeted questions, such as, "Who raised their hand in class?" or "What did your science teacher first talk about today?" a child will be forced to think about his or her presence in class, which in turn can activate working memory.

This process fosters the activation of learned information to be readied for long-term storage. Quite often, you will be surprised by how much a student will remember about his or her school day, when directly questioned about granular details. Spending a few minutes each school day summarizing main subject points and their engagement in class (and social experiences) not only reliably activates working memory but also sets the stage for long-term retention.

Self-Control

By age seven, a child's self-control has significantly changed and improved. In fact, experimental evidence shows that elementary school-age children can perform at adult levels in the context of learning to ignore irrelevant, peripheral stimuli (such as a dot on the side of a screen) and focus on the central stimulus (such as a picture in the middle of the screen). Yes, that *does* imply that your children can put their screens down and focus on the primary objective (as should adults). This means that children have the capacity to monitor and regulate their actions quite well, and while they may not have sufficient experience or consistent abilities to make the best decisions or think through problems, they are remarkably capable of appropriately adapting their behavior to their environments.

Not all aspects of self-control are at adult levels—in fact, although self-control emerges in tandem with working memory, it is slower to develop and therefore can hinder the optimal use of working memory. For example, a child may be able to remember various rules and explain them verbally, but low impulse control (susceptibility to internal or external distractions) prevents their ability to execute and/or obey the rules. Nonetheless, the neurocognitive development of self-control has reached levels in which typically developing children can show the consistent ability to follow basic classroom rules (such as raising their hand and waiting their turn to speak, keeping their hands to themselves, walking quietly in the hallway, putting away materials once the lesson is over, and playing by the rules in gym class).

In recent years, many schools have adopted programs to help children develop self-regulation skills. The Mindfulness curriculum is one example in which children are specifically taught how to develop self-control, awareness of their bodies, and conscious intentions in their approach to schoolwork. Visualization tactics, meditative processing, and related skills are introduced and emphasized at young ages to foster a more self-regulated way of being in all environments.

Mental Flexibility

Elementary school children show improvements in their abilities to learn from their mistakes. During this growth period, they are better able to devise alternate strategies when confronted with problems. Much of this is made possible by the partnership of working memory and flexible thinking: to hold information in mind while working to find different perspectives or solutions. According to Piaget, children of this age range begin to experience "declining egocentrism," which allows them to communicate more effectively about objects that the listener cannot see or does not know about—that is, more easily taking the perspective of the listener rather than themselves.

In the classroom, mental flexibility becomes an essential component to learning and is on an equal footing with working memory and self-control. For example, when learning to read, the ability to understand how the same letter combinations can make different sounds (e.g., "tough" and "though") requires students to think flexibly and not fixate on one rule. Mental flexibility also provides the cognitive landscape to navigate words with multiple meanings, such as "bow" (e.g., "Take a bow for your audience" and "I like the bow in your hair"). Moreover, grasping figurative language and understanding the perspectives of characters in a novel also require flexible thinking.

As with reading, mental flexibility facilitates the emergence of writing. While it is a complicated process involving multiple neurocognitive skills, mental flexibility allows students to organize various ideas and add supporting details while keeping track of the main idea. Checking for grammar and spelling mistakes as well as reviewing their written work to edit and revise all requires the use of flexible thinking. In other words, *transitioning* between all the phases and stages of writing requires the constant activation of mental flexibility. Kids who display rigid thinking may have a harder time shifting among all these requirements.

It is also not surprising that flexible thinking facilitates math development. When solving word problems, students must interpret phrases such as "How many are left?" that indicate subtraction should be used. When thinking flexibly, students can understand and use different strategies to solve the same math problem. For example, when presented with 5+1+5+2, students may choose to add sequentially. Or they may realize that 5+5=10, and 1+2=3. Therefore, 10+3=13. As their flexibility develops, they can also understand how to use prior mathematical knowledge to solve new types of problems (i.e., adding a negative number means to subtract, while multiplication is addition multiple times).

Grit and Growth Mindset

With the reliable emergence of executive functioning skills, the development of grit and a growth mindset become of primary importance during these formative years of early academic learning. In the classroom, foundation readiness skills are reinforced daily. Children are actively developing reading, writing, and math skills. This complex and strenuous learning process is integrated with the skills of problem solving, critical thinking, and performance accuracy. As a result, failure and frustration are common themes. Children not only must have the neurocognitive foundation skills (executive functioning) to assimilate and accommodate new information, but they must also continually be tolerant of the challenges associated with learning. Activating their self-control to remain persistent in pursuit of their goals and showing the mental flexibility to learn from continually failing attempts are central to academic success.

Learning to read is inherently structured as an experience of repeated failure and discomfort until a student "breaks the code" to develop fluency. Students can be susceptible to moments of inadequacy, thoughts like "I'm not a good reader," and intimidation when their friends are toting around voluminous chapter books. As students progress through school, responding to challenges and experiencing disappointments all require the benefit of a growth mindset and grit to constructively weather these moments.

Many teachers and educators have repeatedly asked how a growth mindset and grit can be taught in a classroom setting. It is common knowledge that simply telling students to have a growth mindset yields poor results. Similarly, telling students to try harder can often be ignored. Research has consistently shown that a more scientific and pragmatic approach has been effective in solidifying a growth mindset. Likewise, deconstructing the process of grit and how sustained effort yields successful outcomes has also been an effective process in the classroom.

In fact, with the emergence of grit and growth mindset as heavy hitters to learning success, many programs, curricula, and activities have been developed for classroom use (Go ahead. Do an internet search of "grit" and/or "growth mindset." ... The links are endless). Most activities include educating students and enlisting them in a transparent process of self-reflection. "What mistake did you make that taught you something?" and "What did you try hard at today?" are queries that encourage self-reflection and giving value to errors. Again, it's important to emphasize that the above skills cannot be cultivated without the ability to demonstrate basic executive functioning skills. Self-reflection requires mental flexibility and working memory to recall and compare experiences.

As students are developing a big-picture understanding of grit and a growth mindset, those same skills need to be applied in more granular academic activities. Studying for a test, learning spelling words, correcting mistakes on a multiple-step math problem, and generally approaching the specifics of school work in a self-regulated, measured manner require persistence and growth-minded resilience to achieve success.

Introducing vocabulary, books, and assignments that emphasize grit and growth-minded behavior should be standard in all early education settings, regardless of curriculum philosophies. In addition to classroom experiences, parents continue to be an influential force. Immersion and saturating (but not smothering) a child with the concepts of grit and a growth mindset are critical during these early years. That said, being mindful to a child's sensitive periods of development, for example, knowing the general timetable of when cognitive flexibility begins to emerge will dictate when to introduce and stretch a child's development. Bottom line, optimizing a child's *action potential* begins at birth. In addition to providing a loving, nurturing, and predictable environment, countless opportunities exist to cultivate a child's executive functioning, grit, and growth mindset at home and during their formative school years.

Executive Functioning in Middle School

The cognitive demands step up in middle school (roughly sixth through eighth grades, about ages eleven to fourteen), as content becomes more specialized and complex. The volume and pace of the curriculum also increases, not just in the transition from elementary school to middle school, but over the course of those individual years—sixth to seventh grade and seventh to eighth grade. A similar and even more intense "ramping up" occurs in the later high school period.

Working Memory

The concrete milestones that marked the early years of working memory development have passed, and later improvements are subtler but important nonetheless. According to experimental studies, early adolescents can retain five to seven pieces of information at one time, and their strategies for retention become more complex. For example, they show improved ability to use more sophisticated and efficient memory strategies, such as chunking/grouping, rehearsal, and associative learning techniques (e.g., mnemonics). Although younger children have begun to learn and use these strategies, it is in early adolescence that students become capable of employing these skills more reliably. Despite the efficacy of strategies, the complexity and amount of information taught can become overwhelming to students, as they are just beginning to truly expand and stretch their working memory capacities.

In the early adolescent years, the sheer volume of information and increased density of academic material may appear to outpace and strain the still-developing working memory. From the perspective of educators and parents, the way to deal with this is twofold: to create environments that optimally engage (i.e., not overly tax) working memory and to support the use of strategies that help students make the most of their abilities.

Regarding the first point, many classes such as science, math, and foreign language rely on rote instructional models, typically requiring students to take in and memorize the information presented without context or consistent anchoring to any prior material. While some students readily take in this information with accuracy and speed, this is not always the case. This is not to say that rote learning has no place in the classroom, but that educators should be mindful of the demand placed on students' working memory and use that information to figure out where and why students may get lost or miss information.

Students who feel overloaded or anxious in the face of new information most likely will experience a stress response that limits their working memory space available. Presenting material in a contextualized manner can significantly ease the burden on working memory by providing students with a reference point—that is, a means to group relevant and related information by showing how and why each piece fits together. In math, for example, this could mean framing topics through the use of analogies and metaphors, meaningful word problems, and plunging deeper into the rationale behind math concepts ("In what kinds of life situations would you use the median instead of the mean and why?"). Being able to ease into a topic with a tangible reference while providing humor, patience, and reinforcement is an indispensable framework for teachers to adhere to in their classrooms.

There are also several methods both in and out of the classroom that reduce the cognitive load on working memory, thus opening up more space on the mental drafting table. One such example is the modeling of active reading strategies, which—as the term implies—engages students proactively to interrogate their understanding of the text. Active reading encourages students to ask pertinent questions to reinforce their comprehension and make meaningful connections to the material. For example, even before the first page is read, asking students to guess the topic or intent of a passage or novel will automatically change their focus and comprehension of the content. Students will naturally compare their presumptions of the text to the actual content as the story unfolds. Likewise, reading chapter headings, tables of contents, and brief summaries can all provide anchor points to eliminate overly taxing one's working memory, which can occur when one is doing a cold read of new material.

In writing, the use of graphic organizers can help with early planning, prioritizing ideas, and structuring arguments. Rather than trying to juggle all these pieces internally, having a visual reference of the informational story that needs to be told facilitates the writing process optimally. Moreover, engaging students to tell "the story" of what they want to say before translating it into written form can be enormously helpful in providing an anchored context.

During tests and assessments, students should be encouraged to engage in a "data dump" in which they quickly jot down all the terms, formulas, and salient components of what they have studied, which will eliminate cognitive load and facilitate working memory skills.

Self-Control

Although middle school-aged children are still prone to lapses, they tend to become less sensitive to interference, that is, distractions. However, the development of self-control, like most areas of human development, is not a strictly linear process. In fact, there are quite a few bumps in the road for this age group. In a study in which students across several age groups were asked to quickly identify whether a picture of a facial expression matched a text descriptor (sad, happy, angry, etc.), performance declined among eleven- to twelve-year-olds, compared to younger age groups. While *accuracy* fell within expectation, the *speed* of response was about 10 percent to 20 percent slower. Why does this happen? According to one theory, the cause of the dip in prepubescent performance is a byproduct of the substantial changes taking place in the pre-teen brain.

To appreciate what's happening at this stage, it helps to get a little bit (I promise just a little!) technical. Brain growth and maturation is marked by several indicators, including the overproduction of neurons and their interconnections—called "proliferation"—and the selective process of eliminating unnecessary connections that are not useful or redundant—called "pruning." The process is much like the pruning in landscaping or gardening. By trimming the weak branches, others flourish. By comparison, the sensory regions of the brain undergo proliferation and pruning fairly early in childhood, which corresponds to an explosion of speech, fine and gross motor functions, perceptual and sensory processing, etc.

The prefrontal cortex within the frontal lobe region of the brain, which houses the systems and connections underlying all components of higher-level thinking (i.e., executive functioning) peaks in its proliferation at the onset of puberty. This is when adolescents are also undergoing a slew of other developmental changes. Interestingly, the limbic system, which processes social and emotional information, develops earlier than the prefrontal cortex. Thus, the young adolescent becomes highly attuned to social and emotional information but does not have a stable (well-pruned) prefrontal cortex to manage the decision making that accompanies those moments, hence increasing the likelihood of impulsive, emotionally driven behavior.

Besides having a delayed process of proliferation and pruning, the prefrontal cortex is also one of the last areas of the brain to undergo myelination. Myelination, which a very reliable and easily measurable index of brain maturation, refers to the growth of myelin, a fatty outer layer that forms around neurons and speeds up the transfer of brain signals. Like laying pavement over dirt roads, the production of myelin speeds up the travel of information throughout the brain. Although this process begins throughout the brain in infancy, it is not until the teenage years that myelination occurs in earnest in the prefrontal cortex. In other words, bumpy roads and heightened emotional sensitivity make one moody teenager!

Returning to the prior study about the reduction in reaction time, the complex processes likely explain why the *speed* of performance decreases in early adolescence, compared to earlier ages. Although the brain is rapidly maturing and growing—and functionally, middle school-aged children are much better able to control their impulses and emotions, regulate their actions, and inhibit inappropriate behavior—the burst of synaptic activity (neurons forming new connections) results in variable abilities between (and within) early adolescents. There is a much lower signal-to-noise ratio compared to other developmental periods. What we are seeing, then, is a signal (intended action) that is traveling slowly through an unmyelinated forest of synapses—thus, the slowed response time.

Middle school students are increasingly expected to engage in self-regulated learning, which means organizing themselves to study independently, sit down to complete homework in a timely and proper manner, and schedule and plan for longer-term projects. Related abilities include planning and time management, initiation (getting oneself started on a task), and the prioritization of tasks. Mental flexibility and working memory are crucial in enabling the development and successful deployment of self-control. For example, while a child may be quite capable of sitting down and seeing a task through to completion, if he or she does so without recalling all the necessary assignments, that child may still fall shy of academic expectations.

Outside of the classroom and academic environments, reinforcing self-control abilities is crucial to developing independence. An example is structuring time spent around electronic devices like phones, computers, and video games, particularly as most children tend to get their first cell phones somewhere around this period in their lives—likely much earlier by the time you are reading this! The temptation to get sucked into devices that provide nearly unlimited amounts of mindless entertainment is one that fully developed adults with ironclad self-control struggle with as well.

Another way to foster self-control along with other cognitive skills is through participation in organized sports, either team or individual. For success in these kinds of activities, children must monitor their behavior against the rules of sports, as well as act decisively, quickly, and flexibly to changing circumstances. It means keeping track of moving targets (e.g., a baseball or team members), anticipating your own and others' movements, and coordinating with a team (i.e., regulating one's own behavior) for a desired end.

Mental Flexibility

Building on the foundation of basic mental flexibility skills that have been developed, improvements have been noted in pre-teens' capacity for deploying these skills in more complex situations and behaving appropriately, even when rules change across multiple dimensions. An example is successfully navigating spaces where it is OK to scream (e.g., at recess), where it is *not* OK to scream (e.g., in the classroom), and where it may *sometimes* be appropriate to scream (e.g., theatre rehearsal) without mixing up the rules. Alongside related improvements in self-control that allow tweens to better monitor and regulate their behavior, they can more reliably deactivate and activate the right rules to follow and alter their behavior appropriately, as demands require. Navigating the increasingly fraught social landscape of the middle school years also puts abilities for mental flexibility to work, particularly as it relates to understanding peers' motivations and sensitivities. Of note, some researchers have pointed to an observable regression that appears at this age, returning to less efficient, piecemeal strategies (i.e., thinking less flexibly) and relying on more cautious and conservative approaches.

In the classroom, being able to react flexibly becomes an increasingly necessary skill, as material becomes more abstract and students are invited to apply more complex critical thought outside of what appears on the page. In fact, Harvard Associate Professor Jon Star, who formerly taught math in middle and high school, conducted a series of experimental studies that investigated flexible thinking and math instruction among middle school students. Star discovered that using a flexible thinking model of comparing and contrasting multiple solution methods instead of one method at a time yielded greater and more impactful learning. This is not new to educators, although having access to studies that confirm what is already known lends more power to incorporate divergent and comparative thinking lessons as permanent fixtures within a learning framework.

Providing a daily classroom forum exposes students to broader, more open-ended questions. This fosters discussions concerning topics that do not have a single correct answer, which provide both short-term and long-term skill development. Other useful strategies include the use of questions or assignments that encourage students to consider, for example, what *might have happened* in a scenario—say, among characters in a play or major players in a historical event. This kind of exercise encourages a deeper understanding of the scenario at hand, including how it came to occur and what the direct effects were. It also approaches previously established ideas in a new way. History or stories are, then, perceived not just as a singular, inevitable sequence of events, but as a holistic consideration of multiple forces, many parties, and varied goals.

As parents and caretakers, considerable work can be done to develop this type of more complex and varied thinking in early adolescents, the simplest of which is to engage children in games and scenarios in which they are required to develop and adapt new strategies based on anticipated moves. Examples are classic strategy games such as chess and Risk. Day to day, engaging in self-talk can provide simple opportunities to stretch and expand the repertoire of strategies that children use. For example, children can be encouraged to ask themselves, "Why am I doing this? Is there another way I can approach this that I haven't tried before? What might [X] person do?"

Grit and Growth Mindset

Compared to earlier years, both grit and growth mindset begin to step further into the spotlight, and the impact of fostering these two approaches to learning begins to bear fruit for students. As described in detail in the previous sections, the cognitive resources of working memory, self-control, and mental flexibility form the cornerstone of deeper learning and academic performance, as they are directly required not just for understanding the material itself but also for wrangling the behavioral skills necessary for learning (planning, prioritizing, time management, organization, sequencing, goal setting, etc.). Grit and a growth mindset step further into the picture by instilling the mental fortitude to take learning one step further—developing long-term, internally motivated interests in academic performance and growth.

The relationship between grit and a growth mindset is a critical association for understanding how students frame themselves as learners, their learning environment, and their *relationships* to the learning environment. To reiterate, students with a growth mindset are more motivated to learn and exert effort, and they are more capable of developing the mental fortitude to understand the importance of perseverance. They build a relationship between not just themselves and the material in front of them, but also between themselves and the *process* of learning, including the frustrations and failures that come with it.

The increasing independence and responsibility of the middle school student requires specific cognitive tools to manage academic demands appropriately. However, on an emotional and mental level, they also require students to engage with their beliefs about their ability to rise to the challenge. Most importantly, it is at this stage that a student is developing a greater sense of control over their abilities and learning. Thus, the belief system of a growth mindset moves *beyond* mental flexibility to include an awareness of one's adaptability and control over one's potential. In other words, a student is developing greater self-efficacy.

Self-efficacy is a common term in educational circles, describing a person's belief that he or she has the tools necessary to accomplish a task or succeed in a situation. In a simplified sense, it refers to how *confident* students feel about their ability to wrestle with material and deal with new applications. Grit and a growth mindset are connected here in that having self-efficacy means that students are also comfortable with facing setbacks along the way and having confidence that they will learn from any mistakes.

In the working memory example described earlier, it was mentioned that a student's worry about becoming over-whelmed can lead to a self-fulfilling prophecy in which his or her increasing anxiety can stifle the ability to take in and fully attend to incoming information. At its worst, it can initiate a full-scale fight-or-flight stress response, flooding the brain with hormones whose job it is to constrict attention to the most immediately accessible stimuli at the expense of missing all else. Self-efficacy comes into play by imbuing students with the confidence that, regardless of what they encounter, they will eventually make sense of the information, even if it is not immediately clear. Thus, by trusting their brain, students will counter the negative forces of anxiety and preserve access to their full cognitive arsenal.

Executive Functioning in High School

More than ever, high school students are faced with in-creasing demands for organizational skills, planning longer-term school projects, and managing busy daily schedules. The focus on simple classroom skills and behavioral management has been set aside, with the expectation that students now have the age-appropriate working memory, self-regulation, and mental flexibility skills to organize themselves independently, listen carefully, and seamlessly transition between classes, topics, and discussions. From this foundation, more expansive and abstract skills are built, for example, producing lengthier written work that is organized and structured appropriately, generating inferential insights from text, and making broader connections from one reading to another or to the outside world.

It is amazing how academic expectations increase in such a short developmental timespan! These expectations are further confounded by the often-oppressive stress of "everything counts" for college admissions, which feels precariously buoyed in a sea of rapid developmental currents and hormonal tidal waves. Because this academic stage is focused on increasing autonomy, a student's action potential begins to near its first peak. The harmonious (or often cacophonous) synchronicity of executive functioning skills, grit, and a growth mindset is in high demand.

Executive functioning, while integral to learning academic skills, is more critical to the functionality of school and the daily demands of "doing." For example, independent study, homework, and the completion of long-term projects are highly dependent on executive function processes and require students to plan ahead, predict outcomes, and set long-term goals. Self-regulation and self-monitoring play critical roles in these independent and higher-order learning pursuits, as does cognitive flexibility. Independent projects, a major component of our twenty-first-century curriculum, are particularly challenging for students with weak executive function processes. They involve several aspects of organization, including managing one's time, sequencing information, acquiring the materials and information needed to finish tasks, bringing tasks to completion, and remembering to submit them in time to earn credit.

Working Memory

By high school, working memory capacity begins to approach adult levels. Most notable is the increase in the *accuracy* of the information held. The associated skills reliant on working memory also continue to mature, including improved abilities to visualize actions and outcomes, recall and integrate related information from prior experiences, and plan more effectively. As the complexity of learning increases, many variables affect how information is committed to memory, how long it will be retained, and how easily it can be retrieved. These include the nature of the information, its connection to an existing mental schema, the emotional environment of the information, and the student's level of attention.

Among all the basic classroom requirements at the high school level, note taking by far is the most called-upon skill which students are expected to engage in, despite no formal "training." Note taking is a direct challenge to one's working memory, as it requires being able to accurately hold information heard aloud, process and distill that information into its most important keywords, and coordinate the motor process of writing—all the while delegating attention to the ongoing lecture. As students advance to higher grades, many classes become more discussion-based, and thus, students need to keep in mind both their peers' and teachers' contributions and to successfully integrate salient pieces of information from multiple speakers. Similarly, in reading more complex texts, students are expected to keep track of more details like character and plot information and to connect that information to larger themes.

Likewise, foreign language exacts a complex toll on working memory abilities at this age. While many parents and school programs introduce foreign language learning earlier for students, there are still many students who either begin language learning in middle school or opt to switch languages (say, from Spanish to Mandarin) partway through their school tenure. In addition to learning and working with new rules, phonemes, and grammatical structures, higher levels of foreign language instruction build on students' abilities to produce their own language, for example, composing sentences and short paragraphs in a foreign tongue, attempting to converse with their peers while spontaneously producing language, and so forth.

Assessments, tests, pop quizzes, the rapid introduction of new content: there are endless and obvious examples of how working memory is taxed during this intense period of learning. It is safe to say that a student's working memory is indeed working! Notwithstanding the academic demands, students are also faced with remembering the moving parts of nearing early adult life. While cradled within their parents' care, responsibilities begin to balloon. Band practices, sports, clubs, Model UN, preparing for college entrance tests, and deciding on one's academic future begin to weigh heavily on the precious adolescent brain.

Self-Control

Supposedly, the inhibition blip straightens itself out post-puberty, at least for most students! Teenagers demonstrate improved abilities to filter out distractions and consistently suppress situationally inappropriate behaviors. Yes, this is, of course, a somewhat counterintuitive notion to most. After all, teenagers are notoriously riotous, pushing back against rules and restrictions, seeking risky behaviors, and generally displaying seemingly poor impulse control and decision-making skills: the pinnacle of executive dysfunction! But there are many other factors at work here. Just as cognition in the pre-teen brain is hindered by hormonal and neuronal changes taking place, so too, is the teenage brain.

In conjunction with these large changes in adolescent and preadolescent brains, adolescents and preadolescents are themselves engaging with the world in newly independent ways that challenge growing capacities for self-regulation and self-control. Delaying gratification also becomes a perennial challenge, as the stakes are raised to eat the proverbial marsh-mallow. Should I watch TV, scroll through social media now or later after completing my nightly homework, or study for a test? This can be the difference between optimal and sub-optimal learning and both short- and long-term academic performance.

Culturally, the adolescent experience is defined by social and emotional peer pressures, as well as access to new indi-vidual freedoms, new curiosities, increased and changing desires, other motivations, and self-discoveries. So, what is happening is not a reduction or a regression in cognitive self-control or the inability to deploy metacognitive and regulatory strategies; rather, opposing forces (their interest in an immedi-ate reward and impulsiveness) see a spike in intensity and may win out against their better judgment. In other words, even if teenagers know and understand the right course of action, they may not consistently pursue it. Thus, the intense surge in their urge to check social media, chow down on a chocolate bar right before dinner, or binge on Netflix basically hijacks and overtakes the "you'll regret it" pathway.

What to do? While aspects of what appears to be a regression in self-control are likely developmental, creating accountability and an ownership of responsibilities can often buffer some of the ill effects of adolescent impulsivity. Good old-fashioned employment (summer jobs, anyone?), delegating chores, engaging in sports, volunteer work, church, and activities involving faith and/or community, among many others, can create traction and engagement to offset the competing surge of immediate gratification.

Mental Flexibility

The teenage years are as difficult as they come, but the teenage brain is well equipped with improved abilities in switching focus and adapting to changing rules or perspectives. Bolstered by improvements in the more complex aspects of self-control, the teenage brain can flexibly switch between a central focus (such as riding a bicycle or driving) and peripheral stimuli that may or may not need attention, for instance, road signs and pedestrians vs. billboards and passing houses. Yes, adolescent brains are capable of being good, if not better, drivers than older adults based on their neurological capacities. Teenagers are also better able consider others' perspectives (e.g., think about the consequences of their actions) as well as understand and recognize others' emotions. That said, as with self-control, mental flexibility is a work in progress. As most parents can attest, it is a daily and quite ugly dance between hair-tearing stubbornness and delightful agreeableness.

Within the educational framework, reading, math, and writing remain at the core; however, the expectation is that students can now fluently employ working memory, self-control, and cognitive flexibility to encode and synthesize the information presented. In the most obvious way, mental flexibility is consistently activated during daily class instruction, while completing homework, and/or when studying for a test. For example, seemingly simple cognitive demands such as a student flexibly adapting his homework pace and approach when switching from math homework to writing an essay is imperative to handling both assignments successfully. Likewise, in preparation for a test, a student must consider the type of assessment that helps him or her to determine what information to pay the most attention to and how to properly allocate his or her time and efforts. Being mindful of format—does this student need to recognize and recall facts and information on a multiple-choice test, or is he or she required to understand the basic ideas and themes of a story to write an essay?—is a critical decision requiring flexible thinking and perspective taking.

Reading comprehension is fundamentally the most important academic skill needed in the immediate sense of learning and lifelong functioning. No one can debate the implications of literacy for society, as we often take for granted the daily requirements of reading. Within school, reading encompasses all academic coursework, from dense historical texts to science labs. As previously described, reading comprehension requires students to decode text while allocating and managing their cognitive and attentional resources so they can focus on the *meaning* of the written word in the context of the topic they are learning. Taking this a step further, to process *meaning* reliably and successfully, students need to shift flexibly between retrieving and interpreting background knowledge and attending to and interpreting new content. The goal of coordinating these dual processes is to ultimately integrate known information with new content. This cannot happen without mental flexibility.

As if this higher-level reading process isn't already complex, mental flexibility is also called into play when students must interpret ambiguous words or language, draw inferences and conclusions, and/or process redundant information. With all that in mind (literally), students are expected to prioritize and re-prioritize information to make the text useful for their particular purpose. For example, each time students are asked to respond to questions such as "What was the most important event in this chapter?" or "What were the key factors that contributed to World War II?" they are being asked to prioritize and synthesize information. They are being asked to draw upon working memory, mental flexibility, and self-control to organize their knowledge accurately.

Regarding written expression and writing skills, for students to plan their thoughts in preparation for writing, they need to evaluate and to rephrase or paraphrase the assigned topic, a task that presupposes the ability to think flexibly. Organization and prioritization are also integral to written expression, which needs the crafting of a complete thought that is independent of context and accessible to the "absent audience." Students must organize their thoughts and choose the words for sentences. They must add supporting details while keeping track of the main idea. On top of that, they need to be able to check for grammar and spelling mistakes. All of that requires the use of flexible thinking. Students who show rigid thinking patterns exhibit difficulty managing the requirements of expository writing.

What about math? The same trifecta applies. While there continues to be an ongoing theoretical debate between using a rote mathematics instructional model and a meaningful instructional paradigm to teach math, both systems continue to heavily tax a student's executive functioning ability. Teaching styles have changed to address new math curriculum trends, but these new styles do not necessarily absolve or change the need for optimal executive functioning skills. Rote math taxes working memory more heavily, while the meaningful paradigm forces cognitive flexibility to step up and perform. And both require a significant amount of self-control. For educators (and parents), it remains paramount to continue to foster flexible thinking.

Easier said than done! Examples are infinite and too many to list here. Often focus is placed on seeing the world through someone else's eyes. For instance, teachers may assign an activity where students tell a story from the perspective of a character, for example, describe Gatsby through Daisy's eyes. Likewise, in science, the very nature of hypothesis testing and

Arts? STEM? Physical Education?

Many of you, if you haven't already, are about to cry foul that I have not mentioned or devoted time to the cognitive and emotional enrichment provided by the arts and related elective or special classes. While the scope of this book is narrowed and overly simplified to the core courses in school, there is no question or debatable argument against the enormous impact that music, art, dance, and related special courses have on cognitive and emotional development. A separate book can be (and has been by many) devoted to the importance of creativity, expression, and physical activity to the development of the brain. This is not to be overlooked!

revising one's first impressions becomes not only an important skill for academic learning but also during daily social engagement and as part of evolving into self-reflective humans. Fun activities such as having students pretend to be a red blood cell and then describe their journey through the body can enable perspective taking. And as Harvard Associate Professor Jon Star has purported through his research, enlisting students to purposely engage in multiple math solutions and to flexibly act out alternative strategies keeps the mental flexibility juices flowing.

Grit and Growth Mindset

In the throes of adolescence, it isn't easy to make mistakes, struggle, and accept criticism in front of others. Failure often comes with both a personal sting and social embarrassment. While they are a natural part of the learning process, the pangs still pack a punch. Fortunately, students with a growth mindset and a solid sense of self-efficacy know how to use each failure productively, or they at least try to do so. The personal sting is only temporary, and the next, thoughtful try is quickly under way. The social embarrassment, however, emerges from the interaction between the student and his or her peers, teachers, and others. Building and maintaining a growth mindset requires active engagement and self-monitoring. Dweck says one must acknowledge that one has a choice. One can read about the benefits of a growth mindset all day long, but until one actually moves around the world in ways that fit within this framework, one is not truly engaging in the ideology of a growth mindset. Thus, the most optimal way to actively develop and engage in a growth mindset framework is to create a culture in which students are immersed and saturated with experiences that support it.

The high school stage offers a crucial period for students to develop their longer-term thinking about lifelong goals. During the short period of adolescence, teenagers are shedding prior theories of the world and its potentialities for more realistic and concrete knowledge about the world and who, one day, will be in it. They begin to solidify their interests and have more decision-making power about the kinds of activities they enjoy and are willing to engage in. Recall that one of the key pieces of grit as it relates to long-term outcomes is the foundation and maintenance of *passion* that drives motivation and efforts toward a goal. While children are by nature curious creatures, cultivating those individual passions as they arise and encouraging longer-term thinking and goal setting is one of the largest steps parents can make toward stoking an internal fire for self-improvement and self-motivated achievement. Keep in mind: these interests and passions are not necessarily academic. In fact, exhibiting an interest and motivation to set goals in activities outside the classroom (in the creative arts such as music, theatre, or dance, or in physical activities such as more advanced sports teams and leagues) can build the pathways to turn that same motivation and intensity toward academic learning.

The caveat, of course, is that there is a fine line to walk of supportive encouragement vs. authoritative enforcement. While a portion of wildly successful and talented athletes and musicians credit their parents or guardians for oppressively pushing them to succeed and perform in their given fields against their wishes (at the time), this can backfire for very obvious reasons—burnout, resentment, low self-esteem, take your pick!—and turn out to be a damaging and destructive path to take for the child, the parent, and the trust of that relationship. Rather, Duckworth and others suggest letting children direct where their passions are and, on the parents' end, building reasonable rules about how and when (not *if*) they are allowed to quit or give up. This also saves parents from the unfortunate scenario of dumping x-hundred dollars on an instrument that gets thrown aside for a new one the following week.

It's also perfectly reasonable for children not to truly know where their passions lie—just ask any adult what they thought their careers would be at age 15! To start young adolescence with the process of focusing on short- and long-term life goals and interests, parents and teachers should create opportunities in which students are exposed to environments that challenge them to aspire to greater skill levels (e.g., science fairs/competitions, arts summer programs, sports, etc.).

Essentially, we know that the foundation of grit requires the cognitive ability to show flexibility and self-control as well as the mental fortitude to understand the importance of persevering. How do we cultivate grit for learning? Understanding grit's significant role and its development within learning involves understanding the time scale of persistence. The short-term time scale of grit is an early marker for developing long-term, more transformative grit. Goals of persistence can be considered short-term, such as solving a difficult math problem; medium-term, such as studying for an exam or completing a multi-step science or history project; or long-term, such as graduating from high school and being ready for college and beyond. Building a culture of grit inside and outside the classroom is clearly paramount to our children's ability to achieve success; however, the process to do this requires scrutiny.

Duckworth herself warns against using the Grit Scale to measure individual progress as well as treat the development of grit as yet another skill subject to constant testing. Quantifying grit is valuable at the research level, but it is not a prescriptive tool. Likewise, enabling a growth mindset is not an intuitive or automatic result from experienced failure. Even with adolescents who have been primed to have an optimal growth mindset and grit, they are more likely to succeed when they can draw upon specific strategies and tactics to deal with challenges and setbacks. They need actionable strategies and concrete skills to effectively take responsibility and initiative.

The combination of executive functioning skills and grit and growth-minded competencies, hence, action potential, provides the tools to employ productive solutions under uncertain conditions. One's action potential allows actionable engagement to define tasks, plan, monitor, and cope with specific obstacles.

Chapter 13
College and Beyond

How Much More? Educational Attainment

Action potential shapes how much education a student attains, in both formal and informal settings, as well as how far he or she will pursue learning and growth in a professional setting. In other words, action potential doesn't stop once formal schooling ends. An individual's school knowledge and/or university degree is only as helpful as his or her ability to make use of it. That said, it is undeniable that our brains are at the epicenter of hard times with the onslaught of endless information confounded by what seems like waning impulse control to ignore or selectively filter distractions. We've become Lucille Ball, frantically stuffing chocolates in our mouth to keep up with the rapid conveyor belt of society (*I Love Lucy*, anyone?). The rapidity of technology and changes in our society are occurring faster than in any other decade, and we are overwhelmed. Our ability to stay the course and reach our goals successfully matters more than ever.

Setting aside the complex conversation of whether college and a graduate school education are overrated (i.e., not necessary, appropriate, or financially sensible) for some students, we do have more than sufficient evidence confirming that staying in school matters. We're not even talking financially here; the benefits correlated with longer schooling are clear. A recent report from the Centers for Disease Control found that individuals with higher levels of education tend to live longer, more active, and healthier lives. This is not to say that every student should pursue college or graduate school, or that doing so is the only path to a successful or fruitful life. There are valid arguments that higher education institutions need to evolve and that a liberal arts education may soon become obsolete.

Regardless of our views on modern college pedagogy, there will always be a societal need for the pursuit of continuing education. In other words, we need doctors, scientists and researchers, lawyers, policy makers, nurses, engineers, etc. We need individuals to tolerate frustration to master a level of expertise that will improve our society—and it is clear that one's action potential will determine one's success within that system.

Executive Functioning + Grit + Growth Mindset: Where Are We Now?

Executive functioning, which reaches full development in the early to mid twenties, has now subtly retreated but not far behind the spotlight of grit and a growth mindset. In more applicable terms, where executive functioning skills lay the groundwork for success and long-term endeavors by providing the cognitive tool set, grit and growth mindset competencies are what carry the distance in pursuit of these goals.

Working Memory

As the adolescent now slowly transitions to young adulthood, all aspects of working memory—the accuracy, amount, and duration of information held—have become more efficient, requiring less effort than the teenage brain to retain. A normally functioning young adult can remember multiple tasks, rules, and strategies that they adapt for different situations appropriately. Because of these more efficient working memory abilities, the young adult brain is also better at making quicker value judgments on the merits of ideas.

In a particularly demonstrative and classic study, young adults and children were presented with a simple question: "Swimming with sharks: good idea or not a good idea?" While there was no difference in the content of the response (clearly, not a good idea without considerable protections!), the brains of young adults and children showed activation in different areas, indicating distinctions in the way information is processed and retrieved. The adults, who produced a *quicker* response, did so by visualizing the outcome and drawing that information into working memory, as opposed to the adolescent brain, which took the slower path of reasoning through the proposition. This is not to say that, once in college or upon the completion of high school, young adults immediately activate the more capable and reliable use of working memory; however, they begin to show greater efficacy, speed, and accuracy.

Self-Control

This is a big one. Learning becomes more independent. Students are expected to be able to structure their own learning and organize themselves without the daily interface of teachers, classes, hall monitors, or bathroom passes. There is more downtime and less structure, which requires significantly more discipline and mindfulness. No one is there to tell you when to go to bed, when to eat, when to study, or to when to stop binge watching Netflix! Considering that the neural structures underlying executive functioning do not fully mature until age twenty-five, this is a monumentally challenging period for many young adults adjusting to college life, and for some, it is a "sink-or-swim" experience. In fact, it is a trial run (of sorts) for the rigors of post-college, professional life.

With all the proverbial noise and tangible distractions, it is hard to believe that, at this stage, the young adult brain is much better equipped to display the more consistent regulation of impulses, desires, and emotions. A typical, normally functioning adult is (supposedly) capable of generating situationally appropriate responses, resisting a "tit for tat" response with roommates, professors, and eventually the workplace when confronted with seemingly unfair criticism. Young adults are also better at maintaining focus despite distractions and prioritizing when and how to deal with distractions or other competing responsibilities, for example, multi-tasking. Again, while we have heard and witnessed countless situations in which young adults crash and burn in college, the focus here is on typical development and what we know to be consistently true about brain development at this age and stage. Neurologically speaking, students have more at their disposal, although they likely need the maturity to maximize their capabilities.

Mental Flexibility

In 2016, the World Economic Forum reviewed the future of jobs across nine different industries in fifteen of the world's largest economies and reported that employers will soon be placing more emphasis on cognitive abilities like flexible thinking and adaptability. This trend is not surprising, as technology companies aim to increase individual efficiency and introduce novel ways of addressing day-to-day problems—or in some cases producing new solutions to problems we didn't know we had. This is an industry that is monetizing mental flexibility. As consumers, we can opt in or out of many new technologies or industries as they spring onto the market. However, in many arenas, it is necessary to adapt to new methods or risk being left behind, for example, using the internet as a professional tool (LinkedIn, networking), adapting to new versions of software or hardware, etc.

This is not lost on the young adult who is now faced with choices to adapt to demands in daily living and in future prospects of employment and professional pursuits. While mental flexibility and remaining open to alternative perspectives is a lifelong endeavor, the normal, healthy, and functional young adult should be able to revise actions and plans in response to changing circumstances. In many ways, college has become the fulcrum for students to engage in inquiry, discovery, trial and error, and divergent thinking. Likewise, providing a platform for students to acquire data, evaluate gathered information, and then draw, compare, and revise their conclusions becomes a cornerstone to learning.

Grit and Growth Mindset

Throughout an individual's academic career, more risks are taken as we age. Getting into college, applying for a job, going to graduate school, and failing to make the cut will happen in our lives repeatedly. As demands increase, as we experience more of life, we statistically increase our probability of hard times. Faced with a challenge unlike any prior experience (the jump from high school to college, from college to graduate school, or from high school or college/graduate school to professional life), a person's beliefs about his or her abilities to perform are the key that unlocks or closes the door of opportunity in many fields.

This is a time when grit and a growth mindset intersect and are powerful dictators. Students are now pushing toward long-term pursuits with an understanding that the field has narrowed and interests are more specialized. It is time to dig deep and steer the course toward an endeavor. On the time scale of persistence, this is effort toward long-term, larger-scaled goals—graduating from college, pursuing advanced degrees, and stepping up the career ladder. It is easy and comfortable to stay in the same place, at the same level—to stick with the status quo, say: "This is good enough," and take your foot off the gas. There are more life distractions that seduce us into settling for mediocrity. Complacency is whispering in our ears. And this is where the growth-minded and grittier individuals separate from the pack.

It is clear that those who achieve success need not be the most intellectually talented and academically gifted individuals, but the ones willing to put in the time to work at a goal and persist through challenges, ignore easy distractions, resist the compulsion to stay at a "comfortable" place, and continue to greatness. Let us take the ten thousand-hour rule first proposed by a Swedish psychologist, Anders Ericsson, and made popular by Malcolm Gladwell in *Outliers*, which is as gritty as it gets. The idea is that, to attain elite mastery in a skill or subject, an individual must devote ten thousand hours of practice or study. And not just anything counts for practice—you must put in "deliberate, dedicated time" devoted to "improvement." The notion that it (read: success) only takes ten thousand hours has been largely debunked—but we already know that long-term, dedicated persistence (grit) isn't the only factor at play here. It's one part of a multidimensional puzzle that, once put together in the optimal shape, is what permits individuals to attain long-term goals.

Final Thoughts

The learning model of formal schooling has always been in a state of change, as we discover more and more about how to nurture learning optimally. This state of change has occurred at an ever-increasing rate, all the more so now as advances in technology and research have given us an unprecedented amount of access—not only to understanding the learning process, but also to how best to integrate these findings in the classroom. However, in weeding through myriad trends and distilling successful learning to core elements, executive functioning has yet to take center stage. This seems illogical by our current understanding of learning. It also seems quite striking, given the historical and evolutionary impact executive functioning has had on our survival and development as humans. Given the implications and evolutionary power of executive functioning skills, this neural system is pivotal and integral to learning and living. Likewise, instilling the constructs of grit and a growth mindset as important covariates, it is easy to see how the trifecta leads to an understanding and enabling of one's **action potential**.

"So, do I need to understand the mechanics of how the brain works to be an effective teacher, good parent, or competent student?" Not at all (although, it does help to know a little!). While there are countless concrete and practical strategies that can be implemented to activate various aspects of one's action potential at different levels, grades, and ages (yes, the internet is a good starting place!), ultimately the overall ethos within the school environment optimizes one's action potential through continuously and seamlessly instilling language, strategies, and expectations of effortful learning, risk-taking, and productive failure. Students should be given a safe environment with opportunities to mindfully persevere in smart and strategic ways with the ability to alter and adapt their efforts when requirements become different from one content area to another. This requires an unconditional, albeit flexible, commitment from schools, teachers, parents, and students to adhere to and reward this framework. Yes, it's a challenge, and no school or institution (or parent, for that matter) gets it right all the time. And that is exactly the point. No one gets it right. However, the grittiest and growth-minded of us who are well-endowed with good executive functioning skills will keep trying to evolve education for our survival.

ABOUT THE AUTHOR

Vivian Mougios, PhD is a clinical psychologist with a specialization in neuropsychology and neuropsychological assessments in both children and adult populations. Upon graduating from Columbia University, she completed her doctorate at Long Island University with additional training in neuropsychology at The Brady Institute for Traumatic Brain Injury and Coma Recovery at Jamaica Hospital as well as The Rusk Institute of Rehabilitation Medicine at NYU Medical Center. Through two decades of performing neuropsychological evaluations, managing and consulting thousands of students, as well as advising several dozen schools, Dr. Mougios has been privileged to observe how successful and confident learners are developed and nurtured. Dr. Mougios lives with her husband and two children in New York City.

References

Alloway, T. P., and Alloway, R. G. (2010). Investigating the predictive roles of working memory and IQ in academic attainment. *Journal of experimental child psychology, 106*(1), 20-29.

Anderson, P. (2002). Assessment and development of executive function (EF) during childhood. *Child neuropsychology, 8*(2), 71-82.

Anderson, V. (2001). Assessing executive functions in children: biological, psychological, and developmental considerations. *Pediatric rehabilitation, 4*(3), 119-136.

Ardila, A., and Surloff, C. (2012). Executive dysfunction. *San Diego: Medlink Neurology.*

Barkley, R. A. (1997). Behavioral inhibition, sustained attention, and executive functions: constructing a unifying theory of ADHD. *Psychological bulletin, 121*(1), 65-86.

Barseghian, T. (2011, November 4). *Can everyone be smart at everything?* Retrieved from https://www.kqed.org/mindshift/16647/can-everyone-be-smart-at-everything.

Bartsch K., Wellman H.M. (1995). *Children talk about the mind.* New York, New York: Oxford University Press.

Bernstein, J. H. and Waber, D. P. (2007). Executive Capacities from a Developmental Perspective. In L. Meltzer (Eds.), *Executive Function in Education: From Theory to Practice* (pp. 39-54). New York, New York: Guilford Press.

Best, J. R., and Miller, P. H. (2010). A developmental perspective on executive function. *Child development, 81*(6), 1641-1660.

Binet, A., and Simon, T. (1916). *The development of intelligence in children: The Binet-Simon Scale* (No. 11). Williams and Wilkins Company.

Blair, C. (2002). School readiness: Integrating cognition and emotion in a neurobiological conceptualization of children's functioning at school entry. *American psychologist, 57*(2), 111-127.

Blair, C., and Razza, R. P. (2007). Relating effortful control, executive function, and false belief understanding to emerging math and literacy ability in kindergarten. *Child development, 78*(2), 647-663.

Blair, C., Zelazo, P. D., and Greenberg, M. T. (2016). Measurement of Executive Function in Early Childhood. *Developmental Neuropsychology. 28*(2), 561-571. Psychology Press.

Blakemore, S. J., and Choudhury, S. (2006). Development of the adolescent brain: implications for executive function and social cognition. *Journal of child psychology and psychiatry, 47*(3-4), 296-312.

Bodrova, E., and Leong, D. (2007). *Tools of the mind: The Vygotskian approach to early childhood education.* Saddle River, New Jersey: Pearson Education, Inc.

Buehler, R., Griffin, D., and Peetz, J. (2010). The planning fallacy: Cognitive, motivational, and social origins. In *Advances in experimental social psychology. 43*, 1-62, Academic Press.

Calhoun, J. A. (2006). Executive functions: A discussion of the issues facing children with autism spectrum disorders and related disorders. In *Seminars in speech and language. 27*(1), 60-72.

Camus, A. (1955). The myth of Sisyphus. *The myth of Sisyphus and other essays*, 88-91.

Center on the Developing Child at Harvard University (2011). *Building the Brain's "Air Traffic Control" System: How Early Experiences Shape the Development of Executive Function: Working Paper No. 11.* http://www.developing child.harvard.edu

Coolidge, F. L., and Wynn, T. (2001). Executive functions of the frontal lobes and the evolutionary ascendancy of Homo sapiens. *Cambridge archaeological journal, 11*(2), 255-260.

Coolidge, F. L., and Wynn, T. (2018). *The rise of Homo sapiens: The evolution of modern thinking.* Oxford University Press.

Das, J. P., and Misra, S. B. (2014). *Cognitive planning and executive functions: Applications in management and education.* SAGE Publications.

Davidson, M. C., Amso, D., Anderson, L. C., and Diamond, A. (2006). Development of cognitive control and executive functions from 4 to 13 years: Evidence from manipulations of memory, inhibition, and task switching. *Neuropsychologia, 44*(11), 2037-2078.

Dawson, P., and Guare, R. (2009). *Smart but scattered: The revolutionary "executive skills" approach to helping kids reach their potential.* Guilford Press.

Deb, P.S. (2010). *Human frontal lobe evolution.* Retrieved from https://www.slideshare.net/drpsdeb/frontal-lobe-2010.

Denckla, M. B. (2007). Executive Function. In L. Meltzer (Eds.), *Executive Function in Education: From Theory to Practice* (pp. 5-18). New York, New York: Guilford Press.

Diamond, A. (2012). Activities and programs that improve children's executive functions. *Current directions in psychological science, 21*(5), 335-341.

Diamond, A. (2013). Executive functions. *Annual review of psychology, 64*, 135-168.

Diamond, A. (2014). Want to optimize executive functions and academic outcomes?: simple, just nourish the human spirit. In *Minnesota symposia on child psychology* (Vol. 37, p. 205-230). NIH Public Access.

Diamond, A., and Lee, K. (2011). Interventions shown to aid executive function development in children 4 to 12 years old. *Science, 333*(6045), 959-964.

Diamond, A., Barnett, W. S., Thomas, J., and Munro, S. (2007). Preschool program improves cognitive control. *Science (New York, NY), 318*(5855), 1387-1388.

Dockterman, D., and Blackwell, L. (2014). Growth mindset in context: Content and culture matter too. *International Center for Leadership in Education*, 1-4.

Duckworth, A. (2016). *Grit: the power of passion and perseverance.* Simon and Schuster.

Duckworth, A. L., and Carlson, S. M. (2013). Self-regulation and school success. *Self-regulation and autonomy: Social and developmental dimensions of human conduct*, *40*, 208-230.

Duckworth, A. L., and Kern, M. L. (2011). A meta-analysis of the convergent validity of self-control measures. *Journal of Research in Personality*, *45*(3), 259-268.

Duckworth, A. L., and Seligman, M. E. (2005). Self-discipline outdoes IQ in predicting academic performance of adolescents. *Psychological science*, *16*(12), 939-944.

Duckworth, A. L., and Steinberg, L. (2015). Unpacking self-control. *Child development perspectives*, *9*(1), 32-37.

Duckworth, A. L., and Yeager, D. S. (2015). Measurement matters: Assessing personal qualities other than cognitive ability for educational purposes. *Educational Researcher*, *44*(4), 237-251.

Duckworth, A., and Gross, J. J. (2014). Self-control and grit: Related but separable determinants of success. *Current Directions in Psychological Science*, *23*(5), 319-325.

Dweck, C. S. (2007). The secret to raising smart kids. *Scientific American Mind*, *18*(6), 36-43.

Dweck, C. S. (2008). *Mindset: the new psychology of success.* Random House, Inc..

Dweck, C. S. (2009). Can we make our students smarter?. *Education Canada*, *49*(4), 56-61.

Edgar, D. W. (2012). Learning theories and historical events affecting instructional design in education: Recitation literacy toward extraction literacy practices. *Sage Open*, *2*(4), 2158244012462707.

Edwards, C. P. (2002). Three Approaches from Europe: Waldorf, Montessori, and Reggio Emilia. *Early Childhood Research and Practice*, *4*(1), n1.

Egnor, M. (2007, June 8). *Materialist Neuroscience and an iron spike through the brain.* Retrieved from https://evolutionnews.org/2007/06/materialist_neuroscience_and_a/.

Fuster, J. M. (2002). Frontal lobe and cognitive development. *Journal of neurocytology*, *31*(3-5), 373-385.

Galinsky, E. (2010). *The mind in the making: the seven essential life skills every child needs.* Harper.

Gardner, H. (2011). *Frames of mind: The theory of multiple intelligences.* Hachette UK.

Gathercole, S. E., and Alloway, T. P. (2007). Understanding working memory: A classroom guide.

Gathercole, S. E., Pickering, S. J., Ambridge, B., and Wearing, H. (2004). The structure of working memory from 4 to 15 years of age. *Developmental psychology*, *40*(2), 177-190.

Gillham, N. W. (2001). *A life of Sir Francis Galton: From African exploration to the birth of eugenics*. Oxford University Press.

Gladwell, M. (2008). *Outliers: The story of success*. Hachette UK.

Goldberg, E., and Bougakov, D. (2005). Neuropsychologic assessment of frontal lobe dysfunction. *Psychiatric Clinics*, *28*(3), 567-580.

Harlow, J. M. (1999). Passage of an iron rod through the head. *The Journal of Neuropsychiatry and Clinical Neurosciences*, *11*(2), 281-283.

Hay, C., and Meldrum, R. (2015). Infancy and childhood: what are the causes of self-control in early life? In *Self-control and crime over the life course* (pp. 77-110). Sage Publications.

Holmboe, K., and Johnson, M. H. (2005). Educating executive attention. *Proceedings of the National Academy of Sciences*, *102*(41), 14479-14480.

Hongwanishkul, D., Happaney, K. R., Lee, W. S., and Zelazo, P. D. (2005). Assessment of hot and cool executive function in young children: Age-related changes and individual differences. *Developmental neuropsychology*, *28*(2), 617-644.

Jones, D. E., Greenberg, M., and Crowley, M. (2015). Early social-emotional functioning and public health: The relationship between kindergarten social competence and future wellness. *American journal of public health*, *105*(11), 2283-2290.

Kubota, Y., Heiss, G., MacLehose, R. F., Roetker, N. S., and Folsom, A. R. (2017). Association of educational attainment with lifetime risk of cardiovascular disease: the atherosclerosis risk in communities study. *JAMA internal medicine*, *177*(8), 1165-1172.

Lee Duckworth, A., and Allred, K. (2012). *Temperament in the Classroom* (No. 2012-003). Human Capital and Economic Opportunity Working Group.

Liew, J. (2012). Effortful control, executive functions, and education: Bringing self-regulatory and social-emotional competencies to the table. *Child development perspectives*, *6*(2), 105-111.

Luria, A. R. (1980). Disturbances of higher cortical functions with lesions of the frontal region. In *Higher cortical functions in man* (pp. 246-365). Springer, Boston, MA.

McCloskey, G. (2006). Executive Functions: Definitions, Assessment, and Education/Intervention.

McLeod, S. A. (2018, June 6). *Jean Piaget's theory of cognitive development*. Retrieved from https://www.simplypsychology.org/piaget.html.

Meltzer, L., and Krishnan, K. (2007). Executive function difficulties and learning disabilities. In L. Meltzer (Eds.), *Executive Function in Education: From Theory to Practice* (pp. 77-105). New York, New York: Guilford Press.

Miller, G. A. (1956). The magical number seven, plus or minus two: Some limits on our capacity for processing information. *Psychological review*, *63*(2), 81-97.

Mischel, W. (2014). *The marshmallow test: understanding self-control and how to master it*. Random House.

Mischel, W., and Baker, N. (1975). Cognitive appraisals and transformations in delay behavior. *Journal of Personality and Social Psychology*, *31*(2), 254.

Moffitt, T. E., Arseneault, L., Belsky, D., Dickson, N., Hancox, R. J., Harrington, H., ... and Sears, M. R. (2011). A gradient of childhood self-control predicts health, wealth, and public safety. *Proceedings of the National Academy of Sciences*, *108*(7), 2693-2698.

National Center for Health Statistics. (2012). Health, United States, 2011: With Special Feature on Socioeconomic Status and Health. Hyattsville, MD.

Piaget, J. (1932). *The moral judgement of the child.* London: Routledge and Kegan Paul.

Piaget, J. (1936). *Origins of intelligence in the child.*London: Routledge and Kegan Paul.

Piaget, J. (1945). *Play, dreams and imitation in childhood.* London: Heinemann.

Piaget, J. (1957). *Construction of reality in the child.* London: Routledge and Kegan Paul.

Piaget, J. (1958). The growth of logical thinking from childhood to adolescence. *AMC, 10*(2).

Piaget, J. (1964). Part I: Cognitive development in children: Piaget development and learning. *Journal of research in science teaching*, *2*(3), 176-186.

Powell, K. B., and Voeller, K. K. (2004). Prefrontal executive function syndromes in children. *Journal of Child Neurology*, *19*(10), 785-797.

Pribram, K. H. (1976). Executive functions of the frontal lobes. *Mechanisms in transmission of signals for conscious behaviour. Amsterdam: Elsevier.*

Rimm-Kaufman, S. E., Pianta, R. C., and Cox, M. J. (2000). Teachers' judgments of problems in the transition to kindergarten. *Early childhood research quarterly*, *15*(2), 147-166.

Rittle-Johnson, B, and Star, J.R. (2007). *Does comparing solution methods facilitate conceptual and procedural knowledge? An experimental study on learning to solve equations.* Journal of Educational Psychology, *99*(3), 561-574.

Rothbart, M. K., Posner, M. I., and Kieras, J. (2006). Temperament, attention, and the development of self-regulation. *Blackwell handbook of early childhood development*, 338-357.

Röthlisberger, M., Neuenschwander, R., Cimeli, P., and Roebers, C. M. (2013). Executive functions in 5-to 8-year olds: Developmental changes and relationship to academic achievement. *Journal of Educational and Developmental Psychology*, *3*(2), 153-167.

Ruby, A., and Doolittle, E. (2010). Efficacy of Schoolwide Programs to Promote Social and Character Development and Reduce Problem Behavior in Elementary School Children. Report from the Social and Character Development Research Program. NCER 2011-2001. *National Center for Education Research*.

Rueda, M. R., Posner, M. I., and Rothbart, M. K. (2005). The development of executive attention: Contributions to the emergence of self-regulation. *Developmental neuropsychology*, *28*(2), 573-594.

Rueda, M.R., Posner, M. I., and Rothbart, M. K. (2004). Attentional control and self-regulation. In R.F. Baumeister and K. D. Vohs (Eds.), *Handbook of self-regulation: research, theory, and applications (*pp. 283-300). New York: Guilford Press.

Russell-Smith, S. N., Comerford, B. J., Maybery, M. T., and Whitehouse, A. J. (2014). Brief report: Further evidence for a link between inner speech limitations and executive function in high-functioning children with autism spectrum disorders. *Journal of autism and developmental disorders*, *44*(5), 1236-1243.

Schall, J. D. (2001). Neural basis of deciding, choosing and acting. *Nature Reviews Neuroscience*, *2*(1), 33-42.

Shaul, S., and Schwartz, M. (2014). The role of the executive functions in school readiness among preschool-age children. *Reading and Writing*, *27*(4), 749-768.

Shechtman, N., DeBarger, A. H., Dornsife, C., Rosier, S., and Yarnall, L. (2013). Promoting grit, tenacity, and perseverance: Critical factors for success in the 21st century. *Washington, DC: US Department of Education, Department of Educational Technology*, *1*, 1-107.

Siegel, A. M. (2008). *Heinz Kohut and the psychology of the self.* Routledge.

Steel, P. (2007). The nature of procrastination: A meta-analytic and theoretical review of quintessential self-regulatory failure. *Psychological bulletin*, *133*(1), 65-94.

Stone, C. L. (1937). The Intellectual Functions of the Frontal Lobes. [Review of the book *The Intellectual Functions of the Frontal Lobes*. R. M Brickner]. *The Journal of Abnormal and Social Psychology, 31*(4), 489-490.

Stuss, D. T., and Benson, D. F. (1984). Neuropsychological studies of the frontal lobes. *Psychological bulletin*, *95*(1), 3-28.

Vygotsky, L. S. (1978). *Mind in society: The development of higher psychological processes*. Cambridge, MA: Harvard University Press.

Wechsler, D. (1950). Cognitive, conative, and non-intellective intelligence. *American Psychologist*, *5*(3), 78.

Williams, B. R., Ponesse, J. S., Schachar, R. J., Logan, G. D., and Tannock, R. (1999). Development of inhibitory control across the life span. *Developmental psychology*, *35*(1), 205-213.

Willoughby, M. (2013). Measurement of executive function in early childhood. *Memos on Measures of Social-Emotional Development in Early Childhood, by Subdomain, 200*(2012-F), 43-52.

Wolfe, C. D., and Bell, M. A. (2004). Working memory and inhibitory control in early childhood: Contributions from physiology, temperament, and language. *Developmental Psychobiology: The Journal of the International Society for Developmental Psychobiology, 44*(1), 68-83.

World Economic Forum. (2016, January). The future of jobs: Employment, skills and workforce strategy for the fourth industrial revolution. In *World Economic Forum*.

Zeigarnik, B. (1927). On the retention of completed and uncompleted activities. *Psychologische Forschung, 9*, 1-85.

Zelazo, P. D., and Müller, U. (2002). Executive function in typical and atypical development. *Blackwell handbook of childhood cognitive development*, 445-469.

Zelazo, P. D., Muller, U., Frye, D., and Marcovitch, S. (2003). The development of executive function in early childhood. Monographs of the Society for Research in Child Development, 68(3), Serial No. 274

56112796R00092

Made in the USA
Middletown, DE
19 July 2019